THE LIGHT FROM THE WEST

POEMS BY TONIA BEVINS

Copyright © 2025 Vale Royal Writers Group

All rights reserved.
ISBN-10: 1985794888

Acknowledgements

Printed and published with the kind permission of
Roger Kinsella and family

Cover design by Liz Leech

Compiled and edited by
Liz Leech, Liz Sandbach, Marian Smith
and members of Vale Royal Writers

All characters and events in these poems are fictitious. Any resemblances to real people, living or dead, are purely coincidental. This book is sold subject to the condition that it shall not, by way of trade or otherwise, be lent, resold, hired out, or otherwise circulated without the authors' prior consent in any form of binding or cover other than that in which it is published and without a similar condition being imposed on the subsequent owner. No part of this publication may be reproduced, stored in a retrieval system or transmitted in any form or by any means, electronic, mechanical, photocopying, recording or otherwise, without the prior written permission of Vale Royal Writers Group.

Foreword

Tonia Bevins was already a poet of rare talent when, in 2003, she helped found the Vale Royal Writers Group. In the years that followed, the group was privileged to be able to watch her develop that talent, to the point where she became one of the North West's most gifted, well known and best loved contributors to the poetry and creative writing community.

Those of us who knew Tonia, or were familiar with her work, or lucky enough to witness her performing, can attest to her amazing ability to craft words into something of great beauty that was also inspiring, entrancing and capable of stirring emotional responses that left people amazed and, on occasion, awe-struck.

Always generous with her time, Tonia played a leading part in organising and contributing at festivals, open-mic events, and wordfests across the region, particularly in her home county of Cheshire and the city of Liverpool, a place she knew well and loved, and which inspired her to write some of her most memorable pieces. When asked what it was that drew her to the city, she replied, 'because the light comes from the west', hence the title of this collection.

The contents of this anthology are representative of Tonia's prodigious output over many years. Our hope is that not only will it provide an enduring record of some of her most cherished and widely admired work but also inspire and encourage wordsmiths everywhere, especially, perhaps, those just starting out on their writing journey, to follow in her footsteps.

She is, and always will be, greatly missed.

Bob Barker
Chair of the Vale Royal Writers Group
2025

The Light from the West

Tribute

The following poem was written by Liz Leech and was read at Tonia's funeral.

Tonia

I drove home from the meeting
through a late evening sunset,
blush pink in a sea of orange
that merged into that special
clear blue of a hot summer night's sky
and thought of you
flitting through your garden,
touching this and that bloom
with a gentle caress of your hand.
You were not there tonight,
as we met and shared words
that tumbled and jostled
and vied for attention.
We will never hear again
that coy well-enunciated brilliance
that you conjured up,
well-defined and honed
by your imagination.
You were not there, and yet
you will always be there,
in step with us,
encouraging and urging us
towards a higher level.
As you tripped through your garden,
you will tiptoe through our minds,
call us to book, and we
will try just that little bit harder
to emulate that magic that was
truly yours.

The Light from the West

CONTENTS

Foreword v
Tribute vii
PEOPLE AND PLACES 1
   I Come From 2
   Northwich Under The Skin 3
   Liverpool Ghazal 5
   Northwich Poem/I Always Punched Above My Weight 6
   Howick Hall, September 2011 8
   Sweet William 10
   Autumn at the Villa Cleobolus 11
   Sargasso Soup 12
   West Kirby 14
   Squire's Gate Airport 15
   Loose Pantoum for Will Self 16
   Thurstaston 17
   Excavations, Chester 18
   In Another Country, Soldiers 19
   Freerunners 20
   Camouflage 21
   The Bridge 22
   Red Lights 23
   Tatton 24
   Delamere 25
   Visitors 1st August 2003 26
   Griffiths Road Lagoons 28
   The Paradise Project 29

These Old People 30

River Daughter, River Mother 31

LOVE 33

Lime Street Love 34

Valentine Ghazal 35

Possession 36

Wild Horses 37

Fetish 38

Kisses 39

LOSS 40

Salt and Vinegar 41

The Hunger Says 42

Never The Farm 43

Nothing To Do With Mother 44

For Valerie 45

Ghosts at My Table 46

Helter Skelter Birthday Blues 47

CATS 48

How Tabby Cats Got Their Name 49

Old Melon Eyes 50

Alien 51

Miss Thomas 52

The House Cat 53

Today Is Not a Day for Poetry 54

Before I Remembered 55

MEMORY 56

Patchouli 57

The Light from the West

The Hand Colourist 58
On Cold Sunday Lunch with Recipe 59
The Geologist's iPad 60
At Kai's Beach Bar 61
At Bamburgh 62
Shalimar and Ether 63
The Archaeology of Tiramisu 65
Passerine 66
Like Mother, Like Daughter 67
Hair (1969) 69
Provincial 70
Slow 72
Dog Tag 73
Blood Moon 76
Silkweed 77
Time 78
Durban 79
O'Connell Street 1963 80
Cod 81
Finishing School 82
Long Grass Sundays 83
The Drawer Less Opened 85
Island 86
Margarethe 88
Guttering 90
For George 91
Pink 92

Rollmops 93
HUMOUR 94
   One Night an Iris 95
   In Which I, Arturo, Am Likened to an Artichoke 96
   Heigh Ho, Silver 98
   Harajuku Lovers 101
HISTORY 102
   On Shakespeare's 450th Birthday 103
   Tzarina 104
   Russian Caravan 105
   Mary Miller 107
   The Ballad of 'Lucky' Tower 109
   Isle of the Cross 111
   The Shadow Flyers 113
   Journey of the Pilgrims 114
   1000 Lashes 116
NATURE 117
   Sprawl 118
   Waiting for Rain 119
   Pantoum For Autumn 120
   Lotus Eating 121
   Starlings 122
   Common Weeds Cut-up 123
   Puffball Roulette 124
   Protea 125
   A Pact 126
   Conman Autumn 127

    For St Elmo 128
    Come November 129
    Winter Sleepwalking 130
ART 131
    River Irwell Time 132
    Jazz 133
INTROSPECTION..134
    Something of the Night 135
    Message From McNaught 137
    No Lullaby 138
    Jubilo 139
    The Divided Night 141
    Loops 142
    The Spaces In Between 144
    Audit at the Breakfast Bar 146
    No Thrills 148
    Cold War 149
    Explorers 150
    Escape Plan 152
MISCELLANEOUS..154
    Red Coyotes 155
    Swallow Diver...157
    Flerovium (Ununquadium) Periodic Number 114 159
    Small for the Average Woman.....................................160
    Mercy's Manikin 162
    Three Riddles 163
INDEX 164

PEOPLE AND PLACES

I COME FROM ...

(after Imelda Maguire)

I come from soft sand and wide skies,
the tidal slop of sing-song tongues, from coastal people
who, when land-locked, couldn't help themselves,
fetched up in ports, salt water pulsing through their veins,
who followed the silver, weaving in and out,
slipping over borders like elvers or smolt:
a line of reivers, fishers, a brace of doctors, a furrier,
a farmer-poet with some land and the one slim volume.

I come from small towns and provincial cities,
the fingerlings of children sent away too soon
to sink or swim far from Cork, Dundee and Dragør,
those juveniles who never really left at all,
striving like salmon home to spawn.

I come from children born to mothers, fathers
who died too young from accidents and tumours,
their fates mouthed out in dumb-show
by thin-lipped old women in closed-curtained parlours.

The Light from the West

NORTHWICH UNDER THE SKIN

I am your taxi-driver peddling knock-off cigarettes,
the pensioner beside you in the pet shop
after a harness and lead for the ferret.
I am the old biker lady, all studs and chains,
crumpled white face above a black leather vest.
I am the hamster brought out unhurt from the blazing flat,
supplying your all-time favourite headline.
I am the tattooed man, every visible inch of skin inked out in green:
I forgive your gob-smacked stare each time you see me.
I am the one-armed man sweeping litter in the park,
the ones 'going Tesco', 'going Bingo',
because who wastes a preposition these word-strapped times?
I am the drama queen on the midnight skyline,
the stage-set chemical plant fizzing in the limelight.

I am the fast-food joints and 'We Buy Gold',
the nail bars, pound stores and boarded-up pubs.
I am the underbelly, the unprovoked attack,
five against one outside the chip-shop
on a street that's dead by 9.00 p.m.
I am the old merchants' subdivided villas,
the new all-day-lonely dollhouse estates.
I am sixties civic concrete and jacked-up black-and-whites,
blue bridges, meanders and graceful flights of locks.
I am long, secret lanes leading nowhere,
aspirations thwarted and hopes dashed.
I am coarse and salty, I give you that sinking/rising feeling,
your sliced white going round all night:
you breathe in the aroma as you skim the bypass,
finding yourself ravenous for toast.

I am the reek of drains invading your nostrils
where streets run down to the river.
I am tight enough you're on nodding terms with strangers.

The Light from the West

I have edged out far enough into a hinterland
of hamlets and business parks to retain my mystery.
I am every northern town, yet like no other.
I am the one you know in your bones like a long-lost sister,
the one you sometimes don't know at all,
the one you defend but haven't earned the right to mock,
the one you'd weep for if you could ever leave.

LIVERPOOL GHAZAL

What is this bay, this river mouth, this port, this Liverpool,
Spring Anchorage lipped on the green pool of Liverpool?

On the Atlantic suck and spit of tides, the gathered in
and the outcast drift; the past, so casually cruel to Liverpool.

The Garston bus, early doors in empty bars still bring you back.
I was your plaything for a while, your fool in Liverpool.

On Hardman Street Somali women smile and traffic slows;
in rainbow jalabeeb they glow like jewels in Liverpool.

These sledgehammer hot nights music spills through open windows;
salsa, dancehall, Elgar, rock 'n' roll – so cool in Liverpool.

Billy Fury, teen idol, I wish you'd stayed in Dingle.
London unlaced your soundtrack from the spool, its Liverpool.

Banana box tarantulas scuttle from the docks by night:
urban myth or truth? Send Java plums, sweet jambul to Liverpool.

City of dreamers, where fortunes wax and wane like the moon,
keep one eye on the horizon is the rule in Liverpool.

Your stowaway poet, incomer, incast, fears exile
with sea monsters in Ultima Thule – ah, Liverpool.

NORTHWICH POEM / I ALWAYS PUNCHED ABOVE MY WEIGHT

Once I was Witton, little settlement in the woods.
I watched Vikings maraud the River Weaver.
Now windblown gulls raid my landfills.

I'm your tart with a heart, always reaching out
to neighbouring towns – I'm moving in
on Chester, Warrington, Runcorn, then on to Liverpool.

But my children stay close, seldom marry out.
You can see my face in our generations, a look
passed on down the ages.

I worry for my daughters, some over-thin and under-clothed,
padded bras and whale-tails exposed – too young
to push buggies through my wind-tunnel streets.

As for me, I'm worn out. My stays slip, my shoulders droop.
My shops die in the night. Pity my haphazard rooflines,
swaybacked like old carthorses.

Yet wonder at my black and whites!
Lift your gaze and marvel at my jetted windows,
my corbels and finials, my painted carvings.

They called me 'wych' for salt-town and I was rich with it,
the sharp edge, the grit under winter foot and wheel.
Explore my crystal caverns, my brine lagoons, my meres and
flashes.

Ignore lush ferns and trash gathering in my dank clefts.
I am comfortable as a battered sofa, a soft mattress
shedding feathers, a carpet slipper, down on my uppers.

The Light from the West

You might wander my parks, my green towpaths in pyjamas,
I would never bother you, familiar as I am with the oddball,
the embattled, the out of kilter.

I am earthy, down to earth but not earthbound.
My breath smells of warm meat pies, a hint
of backed-up drains after summer storms.

But my sound is an endless murmured conversation –
pat a stranger's dog or smile, you'll get a story.
I am garrulous and in no great hurry.

HOWICK HALL, SEPTEMBER 2011

(for Roger Kinsella)

Your mid-life specs lend an academic air –
Classics, Medieval History perhaps.
And sometimes I catch you wool-gathering,
this drift a family trait we share.
But you don't fool me, dear coz,

You wear your car like a sleek second skin,
at ease in the machine, a man who knows
where he's going and where he's been.
Speeding North I feel cocooned,
tied by blood and our mothers' roots
to a hinterland of B-roads and walled fields;
ancient milestones, semaphore signposts
leading me down the back lanes of memory
to Alnwick, Craster, Dunstanburgh …
Each name a reminder of late summer days
spent on this gleaming coast.

At Howick, in the gift of honeyed light,
the air soft and clear, the leaves just on the turn,
we crunch the half-moon of gravel,
approach the derelict grandeur of the Hall,
feeling the embrace of its still living wings:
'Yes, this'll do for the ancestral pile.'
'But however would we heat all those rooms?'

If you were architectural, you'd be the keystone,
unseen linchpin, stanchion, footing,
shoring up the family foundations.
You'd be the crucial joist, brace or buttress,
underpinning what remains of the edifice,
as others, more flamboyant than you,

The Light from the West

flaunt their fancy plasterwork,
their finely proportioned windows.

You're the quiet keeper of the nuts and bolts,
the knowledge of how and why things work – or don't,
the steady taker of the long view.

We stroll in formal gardens then wander off
through rougher grass. Was there a brick-built ice house,
teaming fish ponds once, on the edge of the woods,
close by this gunnera shaded burn?

On the rickety bridge, you turn a rusted iron wheel.
Sluice gates groan, grind slowly open,
releasing all that pent green water.

Charles, 2nd Earl Grey, lived at Howick Hall, Northumberland in the eighteenth and nineteenth centuries. He is said to have valued his happy marriage, his fifteen children, his home with its trees and gardens so close to the sea, far more highly than politics, art, and the fashionable London society of the day. He was Prime Minister from 1830 to 1834, and the famous bergamot-flavoured tea which takes his name was specially blended for him by a Chinese mandarin. Sadly, the Greys, being unbusinesslike, failed to register the trademark and as a result his descendants have never received a penny in royalties.

SWEET WILLIAM

Lately I am haunted by a man
who looks at me then vanishes from view
as with a ship that slipping our horizon,
passes into blue. Or dew that steams
from grass as death unmists a looking-glass;
on silent feet a cat who comes at night
in sable coat, white pickadill at throat.

My phantom wears a ring of gold – a glint
that draws the eye to eyes that burn. And yet
his touch and breath felt cold upon my skin –
we cupped a flaring match against the wind.
I watched him alighting from the ferry boat
then lost him on the teeming bridge of Avon.

Have you seen Sweet William?

In the Chandos Portrait, WS wears a single earring.

AUTUMN AT THE VILLA CLEOBOLUS

Rhodes Town, 1981

I wander among eucalyptus,
through the silence of the grove, the dry graves.
Sickle leaves fall on toppled headstones,
the Ottoman dead lie long forgotten.
Wild lilies, crushed anthemis overspill
the path to Durrell's matchbox villa.

I'd imagined a place at his painted table,
beneath this ancient baobab, settled
in the bosom of his brilliant friends,
having read the books to drink his wine,
inhale his smoke, beguiled
by brittle, starlit talk.

Or at least to eavesdrop,
observe him back in early middle age
sitting in the tree's deep shade,
taking coffee with the mufti, his landlord,
after the war. But get instead

the thwack of tennis ball on catgut, the ghost
of Bunny or somesuch calling out
I say, jolly good shot!
from the ex-British consulate next door.

I rattle Durrell's peeling shutters,
peer through grilles filigreed by spiders.

The Light from the West

SARGASSO SOUP

Once there were horses, jettisoned
when fresh water ran low.
Shark, barracuda fed on their flesh, bones falling from sunlight,
to lie with sailors' skeletons, galleons wrecked off Bermuda,
the shifting, sliding coasts of Florida.

We measure the rate of dissolution, the soft rot
of wooden ships gone to the bottom,
swim among shoals finning in and out
through buckled portholes, the ghostly cabins of derelicts,
dive deep to retrieve cannon shot and Spanish plate.
Such slow-leaching stuff.

But while you lay lost in love
beneath some moonlit midnight pier,
you didn't miss your plastic comb
as it slipped from pocket to sand,
didn't hear the tide summon it
to join the stately flotsam waltz,

the widening North Atlantic Gyre
where things do not fall apart
but coalesce, massing like candyfloss spun on a wand,
a thousand-foot helix, an undersea column
of plastic floats, nets to drown and strangle petrels, dolphins;

and on the ocean surface, an undulating carousel,
a slop of teething rings and rattles, flip-flops, trainers,
the spilled guts of containers all the way from China,
going nowhere in the Horse Latitudes.

The Light from the West

But the biter will be bit.
We lay down a new archaeology, not of beads and potsherds
but a sea-midden of plastic nurdles, mermaids' tears,
eternal polymers broken down by light to a seabed sludge,
molecular poison to plankton and bottom-feeders.
Such as us.

WEST KIRBY

Let there be just one gullible stranger,
one who's never been here before,
not in on the trick, the miracle,
one who will gasp in wonder from the shore.

Let him marvel at us walking on water
far out on the shimmery Irish Sea,
out on the edge between the blue and the silver,
just me and you, just you and me.

Let him rub his eyes in disbelief
at our silhouettes, back-lit, sharp against the sun,
gesticulating, deep in conversation –
on our way to visit selkies and hermits.

SQUIRE'S GATE AIRPORT

A place of licence
beside the floating market gardens of The Moss,
a marshy no-man's land of will-o'-the-wisp
where you don't want to be lost at night,
out alone in the lanes with no one about,
only them as shouldn't be.

A place of detachment
where you can seem before becoming,
where you can loose the moorings
close to the shifting dunes – themselves untethering –
from land and glittering sea.

A place of liberty
where on weekend mornings in cast-off cars
I practise hand-brake turns
as weeds lift the asphalt selvedge
of an abandoned wartime runway.

A place of rapture
where you can take the brakes off and throttle back,
where on summer tea-times I learn about kissing
as small planes like seabirds skim the water,
climbing higher, disappearing.

A place of departures
where we pose and flirt on Saturday evenings
in the Tartan Bar, teenage engines revving up
on pale ale and Babycham,
test our wings before fledging.

LOOSE PANTOUM FOR WILL SELF

I really did meet a famous writer once
in the Reading Room of the British Museum.
We lounged on a sofa right under the dome.
Light like water poured through the oculus.

In the Reading Room of the British Museum
there was some kind of class going on.
Light like water fell from the oculus.
Veiled women brought coffee in styrofoam cups.

There was some kind of class going on.
I became rude and spiteful about his novella.
Veiled women brought coffee in styrofoam cups.
It was autumn time, in the late 1990s.

I'd been loud and vitriolic about that novella.
His leather jacket creaked when he shrugged his shoulders.
It was autumn time, in the late 1990s.
He asked me to drive him down to The Serpentine.

His leather jacket creaked when he moved his shoulders.
We walked in silence to where my car was,
then he asked me to leave him down by The Serpentine.
His eyes shone dangerously ultra-marine.

I met a really famous writer once.
He carried a hold-all spattered with gold dust.
We sat on a sofa right under the dome.
All this took place one night in a dream.

We walked through the rain to where my car was.
Water leaked through the sun-roof oculus.
His stare was a dangerous ultra-marine.
Did I mention his hold-all, spattered with gold dust?

THURSTASTON

You and I walk on air,
bounce on the cliff-top's grassy mattress,
pretending not to read the notices
about what to do if we find a rabbit
in the throes of myxomatosis.
Et in Arcadia ...

Small craft bob like bath-toys on the water.
We consider the slow silting of the river,
the estuary as main artery, furred,
undredged through the fat sludge years,
life-blood choked off from its stricken ports,
the open channels shifting, shrinking,
clay cliffs failing, falling.

Wary of walking too close to the edge,
having lost my moxie long ago,
I fend off visions of foot-holds giving way,
gorse thorns ripping like razor-wire
through desperate fingers ...

Geologist and river-lover,
elemental creatures – shell and bone.
Glacial till, sandstone slippage, lifted by tides,
laid down elsewhere.

EXCAVATIONS, CHESTER

They are digging up Watergate.
Orange tape festoons the trench.
Wear hard hats, high-vis jackets
at all times. Do not smoke.
A carelessly discarded butt could blow us
out of this impossible blue
into the world to come.

I'm dazzled by the glare of low sun,
puzzled by the wisp of morning moon
snagged on unseen barbs.
So I follow the metallic seams
shining on St John's Street's pavements,
like threads of glitz shed from last night's outfit.
Or those sinuous zips that run up backs,
the kind you can't fasten alone
even in a mirror. Man-hole covers gleam
outsize sequins in the road.

Now I notice cellar grilles,
half-hidden doors I've missed
on brisk walks to the bank, the Post Office.
Is the black mouth of the underground car park,
a portal to the netherworld?

In the Roman Garden I watch
a squirrel at his private excavations,
stashing food for winter.
And imagine a minor god of darkness
drumming his fingers, dangling his fetlocks
over the ruins of the hypocaust,
waiting for Saturnalia.

IN ANOTHER COUNTRY, SOLDIERS

In another country, soldiers
wearing desert camouflage, combat dress,
positioned at all the platform barriers
would mean a *coup d'état* or occupation.
But the teatime commuters at Lime Street station,
hurrying to make their homeward trains,
stop to give coins in exchange for a poppy.
One young squaddie folds his beret,
steps outside for a smoke in the rain.
He seems to have recently caught the sun –
a late leave somewhere warm with his wife
or a tour of duty in Afghanistan?
I'm about to ask him where he's been
but am suddenly, inexplicably overcome
by the small inconsequentials of my life.

The Light from the West

FREERUNNERS

They come out of the morning,
swift and silent as Ninjas, five boy-men,
the freerunners: acrobatic, balletic, athletic,
moving, not for the sake of art or sport
but because everything they need is here and within them.
And because they can.

On my balcony I saucer my coffee cup without looking,
think of cat burglars, Douglas Fairbanks, Jackie Chan,
the SAS laying siege to the 'built environment',
a pack, intelligent, cool, working together,
trusting their leader, their bodies, the accidental
spaces of the city, their own psychogeography.

The street below is an adventure playground,
its furniture, apparatus; momentum, discipline
driving them forward, they spring, drop, breakfall, leapfrog,
swing hand to hand across fire escapes and gantries,
traverse walls, like spiders, fingers barely touching brick,
balance on the crests of pitched roofs,
vault ventilation shafts and dormers.

In this game of vertiginous hide and seek,
they are both the hunters and the daring absconders.

Freerunners never turn back, retrace their steps as we do,
do not negotiate an obstacle; they pass over, through,
following their paths of desire to another plane, transcending
the great void in our ordinary heads.

Regretting my own physical and mental timidity,
my jarred joints and lack of fluidity,
heart in throat I watch them leap the impossible gap
between blocks that could be continents apart.
I find myself old and envious.

CAMOUFLAGE

Decades of construction have brought me to love
these green flanks: old branch lines, new parkways, boulevards
gouged out of the land. Saplings that once clung
like waifs to motorway embankments become forest now,
baffle against the hum of freight, habitat of kestrel, hidden
orchid.
In the blur of speed or red-eyed rush-hour crawl,
shirt-sleeved reps and hauliers clock the distance,
oblivious to the no-man's-land tableaux,
deep stands of trees that mask the edge
of pasture, superstores, anonymous estates,
the unreported hiatus between departure and destination.
But I, suspended on a viaduct, stalled between stations,
appreciate the possibilities.

A silenced twelve-bore; the chainsaw's angry buzz;
the roll of industrial plastic in the boot,
the weighted rucksack for that late-night drop
in the lake are all redundant now.
It will be difficult, no doubt.
No light but the stars. A snare of branches underfoot.
The wildwood's bark and hoot. Only the night
to hear my laboured breathing, relief,
as I wipe the spade, remove my gloves,
cover with leaves the fresh-turned earth.

THE BRIDGE

The height of the evening tide
cannot be gauged. The Bridge slides
into mist, its end lost in murk.
The wide Mersey lurks and hides.

We cannot see the far shore.
Welsh hills lie out there, obscured.
Foghorn silent, lighthouse dark;
each mile, journey's arc, unsure.

Red tail lights bead the Parkway.
A barge sleeps on the seaway.
The train creeps into the black,
keeping faith, on track, midway.

RED LIGHTS

China Red brings luck or money
but someone stole her city's heartbeat
while she was elsewhere. Sleeping.

Madam sleeps her afternoons.
Sundown she's up, dreaming on her feet
white flesh spilling over back-door slippers.
Worn satin. Bedraggled feathers.

She absorbs the dusk. Ten minutes.
Red lights climb the deepening sky.
Red lights flicker on the freeway above.
Dreams leave with businessmen in limousines,
an exodus of briefcases, slim valises.
Fat jets carry them east across time zones
to vaults on guarded islands, ranches the size of countries'
fantastical cities: Tokyo Chicago Paris Bonn.

The electricity tricks on. In her parlour window
Madam's red silk lampshade grows enormous –
translucent, tasselled like a medusa.

Do the businessmen look down
or do they miss her sleight of twilight –
a red dragon kite with long streaming tails
a red cloud-trailing hurricane moon –
caught in dark trees, luminous on Nowhere Street.

TATTON

Because winter is long and I am earthbound,
I fall into the unseen mire, a liquefaction
of the soul, even of the heart itself
like the mud left behind in a pumped-out basement.

I step into an unseen mire, a liquefaction –
out walking here, seeking nature raw, unmanaged,
not the mud left behind in a pumped-out basement.
The big house slides in and out of view.

Out walking here, wanting nature raw, unmanaged,
I am taken in by artifice, these shifting perspectives,
the big house gliding in and out of view,
an angler's green umbrella floating on lake-mist.

I am taken in by artifice, these shifting perspectives
fallow deer graze the dreaming parkland,
an angler's green umbrella floats on lake-mist,
a man whistles his gun-dog out of the water.

Damp sheep graze the dreaming distance –
imagine milady shepherdess slipping from the picture.
A man whistles his gun-dog out of the water,
hikers adjust rucksacks outside the cafeteria.

Imagine milady shepherdess slipping from the picture –
an assignation in the orangery, folly in the palm house.
Hikers adjust their rucksacks outside the cafeteria,
I read the paper, take my coffee in the courtyard,

plan an assignation in the orangery, folly in the palm house,
a readjustment even of the heart itself.
I read the paper, take my coffee in the courtyard.
Winter is long and I am earthbound.

DELAMERE

Not long off the plane, your body still in the pull
of another time-zone, we set out for the hill fort,
the climb claggy underfoot after rain.

I lag wrong-footed in sandals, make much
of stretching my eyes across the Cheshire Plain,
watch the darting, swooping martins, the froth
of creamy blossom drifting, the almost perceptible
velveting of foxgloves, tender spears sheathed within.
And the slow assimilation of an old plough
as it buries itself in rich red earth.

You are so good for my late education!
Today our focus will be mainly on sandstone:
shallow seas, glaciers and sedimentation
spanning aeons of geological time.
Sandstone, crumbling like biscuit between our fingers.
All those hefty town halls and cathedrals ...

VISITORS 1ST AUGUST 2003

All morning on our sweating streets
I noticed them, and they were many,
our paths crossing
as they shunned our baking pavements,
kept to the shade of our ancient walls,
not seeking out the sun.
Quiet subtle invaders they are welcome.
In well-walked leather sandals
they slip softly down our footworn alleys,
provincial, modest, blending in.

I wanted to accost them,
ask their secret, 'Excuse me,
is it a Spain of the mind
you carry with you as you travel
so self-contained, so at home?'

Then I saw it.
Our cathedral city or theirs,
as it could be, Cartagena:
Roman, Viking, mediaeval,
riverine – it makes no difference.
They are treading familiar paths.

Later, in the windless stillness
dreaming of triremes and longships
as swans and rowing eights
beat the broad river,
I see them again – a couple this time,
not young, holding hands,
murmuring together beneath the willows,
not seeking out the sun.
They pass a compatriot, a solitary man,
nod 'Hasta luego'
and I become the outsider.

The Light from the West

A breeze reveals the yellow undersides
of leaves, a chip tray skitters across our path.
I reach the bridge ahead of them. Stop.
Below the embankment, trapped by a stanchion
a pool of foul water collects polythene bags,
lager cans, fag ends against the revetments.

And the river reeks in the August heat
and against my will I'm embarrassed,
hope they won't linger,
notice this odour, this eyesore.
And I want to turn, say 'Excuse this.
Sorry for the stink, the careless litter.
But then you know, don't you,
the river smells in summer?
Because it's yours,
as it could be, Cartagena.'

GRIFFITHS ROAD LAGOONS

Let me take you, reader, down the lane
that runs by Griffiths Road Lagoons – a contradiction
in the imagination – Griffiths Road suggesting daily grind,
yet lagoons says lazy, seductive, tropical.
Do you feel a pineapple cocktail coming on?
Are you wearing your sarong?

These are not the turquoise shallows of a coral atoll,
but reservoir beds of waste lime.
Look at the high banks holding it all in,
the Danger: Keep Out signs, the lifebelt on its pole.
If, out heedlessly walking, we should fall in,
would we drown? Or burn, consumed like the plague dead?

Notice the curious lie of the land, how it stretches out
to pumping stations, donkey engines,
derricks that move like chessmen in the night,
the network of pipes criss-crossing fields.
We could be in Texas wildcatting for oil, not brine.
Can you hear the distant motorway hum?

These margins, neither town nor country – a scattering
of houses marooned between boatyard and late-night Spar,
chemical steam clouds drifting across gardens,
a little light industry on the doorstep, fork-lift repairs,
coast-to-coast removals.

And behind barbed wire
the black-faced sheep from Limekiln Farm
seem velcroed to the steep sides of the lagoons.
Do they dream of the tidal marshes of Wirral
as they wait in the rain for their lambs to come?

THE PARADISE PROJECT

Liverpool One Retail Development

It's 6.15: seagulls wheel above a shifting skyline.
I might be in Dubai, Shanghai beside this shopping mall
leviathan.
But it's just mercurial Liverpool
in transition from afternoon to evening, summer to autumn,
blueprint to solid form.

The migraine throb of pneumatic drills stops,
the site falls silent, chained down for the night.
I relax, exhale, tune in to sudden birdsong
as a single crane begins to move.

Observing the angles between tower and jib,
the last rays hitting the cab, the lit face of the driver,
I envy his God's-eye view of the river as he swings out
through the changing planes in a game of three-dimensional chess,
moving pieces in empty space,

steel girders, palettes of bricks, concrete blocks,
a Grand Master aligning his pawns, securing his rooks.
I sit in shadow now, watching the city fade from day to night;
the undersides of gulls' wings, their breasts, his cheeks
glow pink, heroic in the copper light.

THESE OLD PEOPLE

With their watery eyes and sunken faces,
they go wandering around the market hall,
carried on a tide of beige and grey.
Who are all these old people anyway,

muttering their way round the market stalls
in search of a nice piece of plaice for tea?
Who are all these crazy old people anyway?
Soon it will be you. Then it will be me

in search of a little bit of fish for our tea.
Pinch-lipped and faint in invisible spaces –
soon it will be you, soon it will be me –
us – sometime ballerinas and flying aces,

pinch-lipped and faint in invisible spaces,
adrift on a sea of beige and grey –
us sometime ballerinas and flying aces,
with our faraway gaze, our ruined faces.

RIVER DAUGHTER, RIVER MOTHER

(for Sybil Sassoon, later Marchioness of Cholmondeley)

She runs through my mind like a great river
rising out of desert rain or mountain glacier.
She binds continents, worlds together,
borders have no meaning to her.
She is confluence of East and West,
river daughter, river mother.
She gathers poets, painters to her.

She carves her passage patiently,
her tributaries stretch into the future.

She travels on, knowing
private reaches of slow green river,
weeping willows, water meadows
on English country house estates.
But Sybil does not laze.
She wends her stately, diplomatic course,
is friend and confidante of politicians, princes.

In flat north light she's cool as pewter,
yet sometimes a sadness lies beneath her surface,
clouds her heavy-lidded eyes.
Loss is not a stranger to her
though many things are left unsaid.

She is mystery, enigma.
She murmurs and meanders.
She is womanly, wears her power
lightly as a swan wears feathers.

The Light from the West

And then the river falls
in cataracts of white lace tumbling over ...
In picture after picture
diamonds flash and sapphires glitter.
Artists try to capture her on canvas and on camera
in all her silken grandeur.

Sybil brings the silt of riches with her,
nurtures architects and gardeners.
She spreads the fingers of her delta,
river daughter, river mother.
At the point of her departure
many things are left unsaid.
Sybil travels on.

LOVE

LIME STREET LOVE

At the exit she waves goodbye to Mother,
runs to the lover, waiting on the apron steps
where I am also watching, mooching, killing time.
But with less anticipation of delight to follow
because a train is a train is a train.

She leaps into his embrace,
arms enfold necks, fingers stroke cheeks.
Bare legs girdling his hips, she covers his face with kisses,
tenderly cupping his chin in her palms, she sings to him
Baby, you are so beautiful.

He pirouettes, sets her down, rocks her, sways her.
They lean in to each other, crooning together,
eyes locked on in a laser beam gaze.

Will they dance a tango across the piazza,
where espaliered saplings cling to thin steel frames,
dance across Liverpool, this humdrum teatime
of shoppers, commuters, poets, us,
the hordes of the unbeloved left outside the bubble?

We give them space, severally and all at once
touched and amused and red-faced and scandalised
at such panting, raw desire.

VALENTINE GHAZAL

We are unpicked, like a tapestry of lies in the night.
Hear the echo of running feet in the night.

One soft glance, a chance remark can spark desire.
You light a slow fuse – then retreat in the night.

If I dream of you – and you of me – we'll meet
on the astral plane. Or the dead-eyed streets of the night.

You appear unbidden in unknown rooms, unreal towns:
haunter of dreamscapes, tormenter – my afrit in the night.

But when we explore the white wastes of the bed
our pulses synchronise, share one heartbeat in the night.

Does this all-seeing moon make me toss and turn,
drenched in sweat and tears? Damn the heat of the night.

The Puppet Master laughs as he jerks our strings.
We dance. And collapse. In slack defeat in the night.

I'm not Paloma but Columbine – no simpering dove.
Cry Valentine, love's martyr, his name, sweet in the night.

POSSESSION

Those gazes long and lingering, our fingers twined,
each hand loath to loose its partner when hands must part.
But truly, out of sight, dear heart, was never out of mind.
Then we were always in each other's arms, the other's heart,
swimming with the symbiotic tide, which in taking, gives release
to both the lover and the loved. Watchfulness is now love's bane;
I tread softly, not knowing what I've done to so displease.
You say you find me kind enough but plain,
too quick to smile at the wit of other men who only tease,
so proclaim all women whores beneath the skin.
Sir, you mistake yourself by insulting me.
When the green-eyed jailer shakes his keys
who will be the first of us to slip these chains
to live outside love's prison, lone but free?

WILD HORSES

We hope for fat wild horses and find them,
deep in the snow-hushed forest,
standing stock still – an ice crystal orchestra –
breathing music on the frozen air. Listen.
The whispering of the stars.

I spill my words.
They ring out, clatter on hoof-tamped snow,
a broken string of beads bouncing
on a white marble floor.

I burn to kiss you but our lips would fuse.
Shush, don't let our fragile words freeze, shatter
on impact like a fallen chandelier.

But I jabber. Believe me,
at these latitudes, in these temperatures, under this pressure
the larches fire sparks at the touch of the lumberjack's axe;
mercury turns gelid; thermometers, car tyres, hearts explode;
steel girders, bones snap like twigs;
fissures split the streets' skin wide open.

Once I walked the shore in winter,
saw the ripples of a ship's wake imprinted
on a sea of glass, hours after she slipped
over our horizon.

When the thaw reveals dropped keys and single gloves
I'll walk the grasslands to watch wild horses
graze new shoots. Then – tuning in
to a cryogenic conversation – I'll hear
one winter's botched punchlines and lost asides
alive on the warming air.
And the insistent murmur of a thousand
expired *I love yous*.

shopot zvyozd – the phenomenon of frozen breath crystals falling to the ground with a tinkling sound

FETISH

Most days you'd stuff them absently in your pocket
with mints and wallet and the keys that opened everything.
But sometimes I'd find them after you'd gone –
not overlooked – their placing precise, aligned just-so
beside your pen and notebook of ideas for the future;
between half-saucered cup and half-digested paper,
the radio turned too low to be listenable, your chair
pushed not quite under the table.

Not rabbit's foot, not fingers crossed, not not-wearing green
but flip-top box and throw-away sparks – your marker
laid down like a counter, your opener in a game with the gods
to wrong-foot fate, to side-step time, to strike a bargain
in the face of conflagration – your talisman,
hostage to disaster hovering on the horizon.

These days I shore up everything before I slam the door,
hope that all will be as is should I return:
the tides running, birds still calling at dusk and dawn.

KISSES

from the first one, the alpha
a winter flame snatched from the air
of an icy Esso forecourt

driving to the coast that Christmas
the way ahead never seemed so clear
I knew we would play the stars

through the passion, the sudden flare
the fire catching hold, the laths beneath the mattress split
the desultory late for work excuses

through the absent-minded, middle passage years
the settlement of flesh, the comfortable fit
the counterbalance, the slow burn

to the last one, the omega
the screens pulled round
your lips so cold

LOSS

SALT AND VINEGAR

Afterwards, I wanted nothing, sickened at the fridge's glut:
the summer berries frosted in sugar, leftover custards fat with
cream
the velvet slabs of bitter chocolate, darker even than your
marron eyes.

Then I needed strong food: the toughest bread made from
ground-up stones,
hard enough to break my jaw, rock salt, sinews and sea meat –
charred –
the dry flesh of storm birds.

Now, I salivate for raw fish drowned in vinegar, sour as my
guts,
my heart, I would sell my soul for one lemon, a jar of herrings,
relish
their dull grey gleam. Or rather, for the cove in moonlight

to feed this hunger on ink and silver, to have held you longer
but wind and tide caught you as you slipped, love like sand
falling through my fingers, returning to the ocean.

THE HUNGER SAYS

strew flowers on the ocean.
What have ashes to do with one who lives

in light and shade, scudding clouds that pass
across the face of a hunter's moon?

The tide's on the turn as I walk down
through steep white lanes then out along the strand.

Specula dance on the water.
Seabirds still hold the blue void around the castle.

A familiar foreign land, this death –
and he is heavy in my arms.

I watch him move between rock pools;
our blithe footprints mingled on wet sand.

Love, I give you to the light, the wind and water.
Travel far, travel on forever.

And the hunger gnaws still deeper
as the last flower drowns.

NEVER THE FARM

It began with one ewe, a pair of lambs,
yellow plastic haybales, a handful of hens,
then a ram, a rooster, the farmer himself.
Soon I bought him a four-shilling wife
and a piebald horse crying out for a cart
laden with milk churns made of real metal.
Though no cows yet grazed the bathtowel meadow
spread out across my bedroom table.

I'd my eye on a cat to keep down the rats
that scurried about in the night.
But life on the farm seemed under control
till the day I came home from school
to the bare table, the folded green towel.

Wasn't I a good girl, a kind girl?
And little Lars so ill, so far from home.
My farm would make him happy. And besides,
wasn't I too grown up now for toys?

If she'd asked, I'd have given, perhaps
my Crazy Mule puppet, my Russian dolls.
Never the farm. But mother thought giving,
like iodine dabbed on a wound, should sting.
Not balm, but antiseptic for your soul.

How I hated her then,
resented the sick boy I'd never seen,
sulked in my room, played sullen at meals.
A week later, when she told me, I cried.
Guilt-ridden. And still missed the farm,
knowing it would never be mine again,
not thinking, as she fiercely held me, of the couple
on the boat back to Sweden.

NOTHING TO DO WITH MOTHER

This year the days fell out almost the same;
a warm April Holy Week and I couldn't banish
that other one from my mind.
The call came at work in the late afternoon.
You should get over. She's in the hospital.
They say it won't be long.

She'd already drifted far off in coma,
her breath coming fast and loud and rasping.
She seemed so small and shrunken as if sinking
into the mattress on the gated cot,
her skin dark and leathery, the carapace
of an alien creature or a cicada.
Nothing to do with Mother.

There was nothing to be done but go home
to pick at supper, fall asleep in our chairs.
I never heard the night nurse call.
At four he woke me to tell me she'd gone,
just as they'd said she would.

And it being Easter by then, we were stranded.
There was nothing to be done but wait,
sit in silence together in the burning garden,
all through that long, long weekend.

The Light from the West

FOR VALERIE

We said goodbye far too soon.
I walk her city's familiar streets, past buildings blurred with rain.
It rains all afternoon, as if set to rain for ever.

Gutters teem like rivers in spate.
The awnings outside Yates's threaten collapse
under the pooled weight of it.

No shelter here. This is proper rain. A great outpouring
of sorrow. The wind funnels in off the water.
Gulls keen and seem to tumble through saturated air.

Summer has been suspended for a while,
this city drained of colour, save the bright umbrellas
bobbing on a sea of grey.

We said goodbye far too soon
but somehow the rain feels right today.
The river will gleam again in the clear west light –

she'll be there beside us, at our shoulders
whenever we watch her city take on
its gorgeous evening colours.

GHOSTS AT MY TABLE

I recall the day we brought you home –
a Manchester warehouse, a borrowed van –
you seemed to take up half the room,

being longer, wider than we'd planned.
Next we found six Spanish chairs.
That's the where and how it all began.

We'd invite our friends to come and share
a blow-out meal. He always chose good wine.
There were romances and arguments, lives laid bare

among the debris. But everyone was fine.
Now the scratches on your battered face
match the lines on mine.

We lose our sheen. You've become a parking place
for unpaid bills and piles of books.
But sometimes, staring into space,

I catch the ghosts of guests long gone,
now I mainly dine alone.

HELTER SKELTER BIRTHDAY BLUES

Woke up this morning, had those birthday blues
Well I woke up this morning, had those birthday blues
Been so bad baby since I got the news.

Should've been kisses, all your fav'rite food
Well there should've been kisses, all your fav'rite food
I'm through with cookin', lost that kissin' mood.

Should've been rockin' rollin' rhythm 'n' blues
Well there should've been rockin' rollin' rhythm 'n' blues
I'm through with music, lost my dancin' shoes.

Should've been whiskey, all your fav'rite booze
Well there should've been whiskey, all your fav'rite booze
So why quit drinkin'? Nothin' left to lose.

Should've been laughter, moonlight on our bed
Well there should've been laughter, moonlight on our bed
Can't stop my cryin' since I saw you dead.

Woke up this morning, had those birthday blues
Well I woke up this morning, had those birthday blues
Without you baby, this heart's one big black bruise.

CATS

HOW TABBY CATS GOT THEIR NAME

In a paperback history of southern Spain
dockers unload a boat from Arabia:
bales of Attabi silk taffeta,
woven in Baghdad.

A man looks at the sky, the glassy water,
sees why Moors call this place The Mirror.
Black sails slacken in flat calm.
The man sweats. The fabric shimmers
like the sea in metallic light and something else
he's seen but can't recall
in such grinding heat.

He sits below the harbour wall, eats sardines,
throwing scraps to the port cats
that mill and mewl
around his feet.

Their coats remind him of the cloth,
moth markings spanning narrow feline shoulders,
some barred with black, like tigers,
others moiréed with smoke and silver,
tabby cats with fur like the sea at Al-Miraya,
Attabi silk taffeta.

OLD MELON EYES

My cat has eyes the yellow of melons.
Once she was plump, low-slung, cobby
her squat bean bag body full of pulses
she would stay wherever I put her.

But now she follows, and her muzzle is grey.
She is insubstantial, light as air
growing lighter every day.

Mellow with fish and trust she lies
easy across my arms, limbs limp
abandoned in a state of yogic calm.

I place her cushion on the table.
Set her down. And move her
as the sun moves across the sky.

This cat of my heart glows red in the light.
I bury my face in the fur of her scruff
inhaling solace when I'm blue, out of love.

ALIEN

She delves beneath the covers, purring,
finds the crook of foetal-folded knees.
How quickly she absents herself in dreams,
my alien familiar. Stretching on the morning,
she holds me in her haughty gaze.
Were I wolf I'd be her slave.

I am cast to please and serve –
a rude mechanical, tossed aside,
inconsequential as a spent mouse.
Now she'll freeze – then chase her aerial tail –
run mad, as if pursued by djinn,
distracted, breakneck, pinned-back ears
tuned to signals from an unseen world,
my familiar alien.

MISS THOMAS

Scratched by whiplash branches, I'd pull on the bell,
hear it sounding in the depths of her bungalow,
turn back through the undergrowth to our avenue
where nothing much happened, but blossom, each year.
She'd appear then, on silent cat-feet, from nowhere,
too light and spindle-boned, nervy as a stray,
calling out to me with a girlish chirrup,
taking the box from reluctant arms.

A fortnight later, filled with sunshine,
I'd return for my boy – a bruiser tabby tom –
find him sleek, serene, his green gaze curious,
as if regarding a stranger. I'd hand her the boarding fee
outside the lean-to, sneak a glance into her parlour –
a legion of cats sat still as ornaments on shelves and cabinets,
or lazed on antimacassared, thread-clawed armchairs,
dozed before a gas fire even though it was August.

Some would say the place stank to heaven –
that signature reek cat lovers don't always detect.
I only remember a deep, dank boskiness
as it slowly composted itself back into the earth.
I didn't know the officer who found Miss Thomas.
And for some time after, the news was kept from me
of the frenzied guests in their pens out back,
her starving house-cats having done what they must.

THE HOUSE CAT

hunting in the night house
pounces on her old cloth mouse, rips out
its cotton wool guts.

In the dead hours her yowl –
primal, heart-rending –
jars me from sleep. She prowls my bed

purrs, palpates till settling
assumes the contours of my breast.
We resonate. I whisper *Sleep, Old Melon Eyes*.

On waking, I find sometimes
the sloughed, white sheathes of claws –
sharp, perfect scimitars.

TODAY IS NOT A DAY FOR POETRY

(after Roger McGough)

Today is not a day for poetry.
The cat is acting the cobra
Hissing at the shredder. Paper
Diamonds drift to the floor
Like poor man's confetti.

Take my advice: shooing
The puss will not conjure the muse.
Let him prowl about your desk,
Abuse your computer. Editors,
Though helpful, seldom purr.

His mog-dribble will leave a lasting
Comment on the page. Why bother?
Get out. It could be worse.
Keep your scribble to yourself.
Today is not a day for verse.

Best put the stanzas on the shelf.
Set aside till the panther sleeps.
No point adding to the bad.
At this stage, a line's not worth
The risk of going raving mad.

BEFORE I REMEMBERED

On the third day he began his search,
not hunting out but seeking, pacing through the house,
howling like something caged or lost;
then a purposeful scouring of dark corners,
the spaces behind closed curtains,
clawing open cupboard doors,
scratching at boxes stowed under the stairs,
staring up at the high trap to the loft,
sniffing at the air for the very scent of you.

And, as if, I, forgetting, my mind too full,
laid your place at table and cooked too much food
whilst making a mental note to tell you
about such and such trivial things.
Before I remembered.

He wouldn't roost on my shoulder.
For weeks there was no settling, no consoling him.
But with time he came to me, became mine
in the changed order of the world.
How long does memory endure?

Sometimes I open your wardrobe door,
free the hostage smells of leather jacket and cologne,
conjure you there in the silent room,
every hair, pore, fleck and freckle of you,
the ridges in nails, arch of ribcage, set of jaw.
For a moment, I can almost hear
the singular timbre and tone of you,
touch the flesh, blood and bones of you.
How long does memory endure?

MEMORY

PATCHOULI

Sometimes in the slipstream of a passing stranger
I catch the scent, have to watch myself
or I'd follow him home like a stray pet.
Or a stalker.

It is catnip to me or aniseed –
medicinal, heavy, not flower-sweet or musky,
(all that perfume-counter hyperbole).
I inhale its bosky wood notes, feel slyly sexy.

It is the elixir of my youth, product of alchemy,
my pass key. It is the smell of possibilities,
sovereign against the clothes moth,
antidote to the venom of certain snakes.

A phial of patchouli oil,
sticky now, dark as molten tar or treacle,
stands unstoppered on my wardrobe shelf,
among old silk scarves I no longer wear,
yet can never give away.

But you have to smell it, body temperature,
to feel its counterculture pull.
Patchouli seeds are small, fragile.
Were we fools to want to change the world?
Did Alice fall down the rabbit hole?
When exactly did I sell my soul
for a mortgage and a pension?

Sometime between Woodstock and punk
we blinked, emerging from our wonderland
to find the Incredible String Band disbanded
and our minds no longer blown by acid rock,
or *Strange News from Another Star*.

THE HAND COLOURIST

I am looking at it, he said, this way,
indicating the negative pinned to his lightbox:
shadows to be interpreted on an X-ray.

I was intoxicated by the kingfisher blues
of a summer afternoon, green dells, a fireball sunset.
These seduced my eye, my camera.

Lately, finding my palette turning sepia:
I capture wood-smoke, seed pods, fungi,
blurring intricate structures through a fog filter.

But my best work, he insisted, is yet to come:
silhouettes of bare black trees; grey geese caught
against a flat white sky; a lake iced over.

There will, however, be hints of colour
which I shall paint in sparingly, less being more.

ON COLD SUNDAY LUNCH WITH RECIPE

Last night's salmon, the tail-end,
my Sunday lunch, foiled and gelid from the fridge:
I'm thinking rye bread, lettuce, mayo
but see my father in his middle age
lift the fish from its steaming kettle,
lay it on the sacrificial salver.

He takes his knife, slides the blade along the dorsal line,
slices down through cross-hatched silver,
raises fragrant flesh from whitened bones,
his high-priestly, holiday miracle.

I bring plain boiled potatoes to the table,
there could be nothing green at this feast of coral
but agurkesalat to cut the fat, the gutturals natural on our lips.
Pass the agurke, please. A little salt perhaps.

I mandolin a cucumber, thin as paper. Salt it.
Rinse it. With palms and fingers squeeze out
all the moisture from it. Add sugar. Add coriander, juniper.
Steep the mixture in white wine vinegar.
Taste it. Leave it to marinate in a cool glass bowl.
Remember the words. Keep the ritual.

THE GEOLOGIST'S IPAD

When you produced your iPad
I thought of Hockney in his East Riding:
flatlands, woods and wolds made vivid, enchanted
as I'd never seen them before.
And that the device is not a thing at all.
But what can it hold within aluminium and silica,
its chips and rare metals, liquid crystal
giving up the pristine essence of a blade of grass;
rock strata, dunes, savannah filling the screen
in the contraction/expansion between
your deft thumb and middle finger.

I remember that lightness of touch
as we hairpin down from the High Peak:
how you can read the lie of the land,
what goes on beneath its sleeping folds and furrows:
the changing course of underground rivers;
the upthrust of mountains, the mineral lodes laid down,
the deep past seeming closer than imagined,
given the advance and retreat of glaciers.

AT KAI'S BEACH BAR

Kai fetches a jug of wine, olives shining in a saucer,
red snapper sizzle over charcoal and a cat dozes
in a pomegranate tree, one paw outstretched,
opening/closing as he dreams.
Sand trickles through my own splayed toes,
not measuring time.

Hunters comb late summer hills,
their gunfire cracks the afternoon, a tin sign
rattles like a theatre thunder sheet,
newspapers flutter in the electric lull,
the kind that comes before a storm.
The wind whips up white caps
on the sea's green surface,

the delicate menace
of a gamelan tinkles through colossal speakers.
Kai turns up the volume.
The theme from *The Killing Fields* fills the beach.
The first fat drops splash into the pitcher:
we run for the kitchen. The deluge brings laughter,
talk of possibilities, deserted islands.

Kai fixes the moment on Polaroid:
our images emerge from the clouded emulsion,
washed clean. We are remade as small, smiling gods
through this gift of rain.

AT BAMBURGH

Late September, a full month before we'd go
the two of us, without my father, to spend half-term
huddled among the dunes, shivering in the blast
that roars off the Urals, barrels across the North Sea.
We can't come all this way and have you not swim.
Don't be such a baby. Get in!

I'd bob up and down in shock then run back,
blue-fleshed, numb, gasping into the embrace of the towel
held up in her outstretched arms, gulp hot, sweet tea from
the flask.
None of this has made me a more resolute person.

I find myself here again but high above the shore
one wild, ragged afternoon – the tiny, determined walkers
far below.
Tankers, container vessels slide past my friend's window:
Inner Farne hangs on the horizon, in and out of sheeting rain.

When I look out, my nearest neighbours are in Denmark,
he says. But I think of the grey seals and seabirds,
remember
my mother, lamed for life yet game to clamber
down the iron rungs set into the Seahouses harbour wall,
her faith in our skipper's grasp as she leapt the gap
to a small boat rising and falling on the swell.

SHALIMAR AND ETHER

Her hands had a love affair with gloves – Marigold, surgical,
soft black leather …
But I adored the long white silk ones; they went snaking,
on and on up her forearms past her elbows,
making for her fleshy, creamy, powdered shoulders,
and I'd wonder how she'd manage to eat the extra special gala
dinner
as she'd bend to kiss me in a blast of Shalimar and ether.

But just before I'd even see her
standing in the doorframe, dressed – or smell her perfume in
my bedroom –
I'd hear satin rustling on the landing
and seven matching bangles jingling and a charm bracelet
tinkling like the ice cubes
in the cocktails she'd be drinking
later in the evening, making me think of the hard glinting
stones
held secure by small gold claws,
then set into the rings on – most of – her fingers
and I'd wonder, as she was about to leave:

Why does she wear these things
on the outside of her gloves?
And will she take it all off for the meal?
And put it in a neat pile beside her plate on the table?
And what if there's stuff you have to eat with your hands?
And suppose her fingers get all messy?
And she doesn't have time to lick them clean
before someone asks her for a dance between courses
when she's meant to be wearing her gloves for dancing
since all men's hands are dirty and sweaty?
Or so she keeps saying.

The Light from the West

Yet, sheathed and shimmering in her sequined ball dress
she'd dazzle me like Shirley Bassey on the telly
singing *Diamonds Are Forever.*
Forever. As mother always told me.

THE ARCHAEOLOGY OF TIRAMISU

Our waitress, friendly, Scouse with hints of L.A.
chirps a world of exclamation marks and easy familiarity.
We exchange glances, grin. Sweet girl, she thinks
we're Darby and Joan out on the town for a treat.
Or brave second chancers risking a date.

How could she know I've not moved far
while you inhabit another hemisphere?
Or that your eyes, heavy-lidded, greenish-blue,
still incurably amused, are the same eyes
that first drew me to you?

We order a platter of antipasti – nothing too spicy.
You tell me of Africa and a man who wouldn't
look you in the eye till you asked him to.
And I wonder if old lovers can still hold
each other's gaze across a table,
see the past without a pang
of might-have-been?

Later, we spoon our way
down through the layers; the dusting of cocoa,
the froth and soft mascarpone cream
to the core, the heart of the matter,
the raison d'être; bitter-sweet, the ladies' fingers
soaked in espresso and strong Marsala wine.

How mellow we are these days!
How far we've come!
Sharing pudding in a flash city restaurant
from a dish of frosted glass.

PASSERINE

She'd touch down between
London and Dublin, overnighting
in our spare room, Aunt Paddy,
the passerine, never settling,
always leaving,

leaving in her perfumed wake
a négligée, a scarlet lipstick,
a pair of size seven six-inch heels.

My mother called her careless.
But knew she did it on purpose,
certain I'd find the Little Black Dress,
so classic-chic, so Audrey Hepburn,
dream my cow-licked pudding bowl
up into her sleek black chignon.

They wouldn't let me go to the service
and I could never ask who lay in the coffin,
her plane from Rome having gone to the bottom.

LIKE MOTHER, LIKE DAUGHTER

I'm starting to look like you,
even though I swore I never would.
Imagine the shock of catching your reflection
having thought you'd gone for good.

Even though I swore they never would,
sharp cheekbones soften, the jawline slackens.
Having thought you'd gone away for good,
shadows of doubt drift across the retina.

Sharp cheekbones soften, the jawline slackens.
This year I'll be as old as you ever were.
Shadows of doubt drift across the retina.
I hate the way you stare from unfamiliar mirrors.

This year I'll be as old as you ever were.
Hair falls lank like when you gave up the perm.
I hate the way you stare from unfamiliar mirrors.
Turning to look I always find you there.

Hair falls lank like when you gave up the perm.
Travelling alone through the blackness of fields,
I turn to look out and find you there,
blurred in the thickness of a plexi-glass window.

Travelling alone through the blackness of fields
you're always beside me on late-night trains,
trapped in the thickness of a plexi-glass window,
just beyond reach. Is this what death does to us?

You're always beside me on late-night trains,
in public buildings, other people's hallways,
just beyond reach. Is this what death does to us?
I am gaining on you. Against my wishes.

The Light from the West

In public buildings, other people's hallways,
imagine the shock of catching your reflection.
I am gaining on you against my wishes,
starting to look like you.

HAIR (1969)

In Lancashire, rumours have reached us
of Swinging London and the West Coast counterculture.
I am curious but hide it well behind a sullen mask.
SEX DRUGS NUDITY harrumphs the *Express*.
But Mum and Dad and their baby-boom daughter,
with volcanic skin and lank, schoolgirl bunches,
hit the road south one late summer Friday
to storm the citadel of debauchery.

At the Shaftesbury there are surprise tickets
for the notorious American musical *Hair*.
We are so adventurous. All of a sudden.
They pretend to enjoy it – of course, not getting it at all.
But I am entranced, pronounce it *really fab*
while at the same time feeling
even more awkward and squirmy than usual
on account of *them* being there.
And the nudity.
And refuse to get up and dance on stage
with the cast at the end like almost everyone,
even though *they* are shooing me forward –
Go on. Go on. Don't mind us.

But the best is yet to come –
an appointment at the salon of Vidal Sassoon.
A man has never cut my hair before
and though I'm not at all sure it really is Vidal
(who is perhaps out there in Hollywood, styling movie stars),
someone snips away at the kinks and cowlicks
until I have *architectural structure* in my life.

I shake my head from side to side,
the long bob, whispering *swish/swish* as it falls away,
geometric from cheekbones to shoulders.
And I feel so new and shiny. Free at last.

PROVINCIAL

In the morning, because I cried, you called me provincial,
a silly little girl from the sticks, you said.
I turned my back so you couldn't read my face, my fury.
And because I'd fooled myself I loved you.

But soon I was away, thinking about the Romans in Britain,
not the controversial play which hadn't yet been written,
not even the common soldiery, slogging mile after mile
up and down those unswerving roads, the poor sods drafted in
from softer provinces of empire.

How you must have felt for them in exile –
stomping and shivering, blowing on chilblained hands
as they scanned our wind-scoured borderlands
from their forts along The Wall.

And all the while worrying about keeping the lid on
the mad red barbarians to the north,
the double-dealing blue barbarians to the south.

So not those Romans –
who wouldn't have been here given a choice –
but rather men like you,
who thought it was alright to drone on and on
about our general lack of sophistication and central heating,

men like you, the governors, with dead eyes and smooth
Hampstead ways,
men like you who could improvise cool jazz piano solos in
basements,
all weeping candles rammed into old Chianti bottles,
men like you with too many glottal stops and lazy metropolitan
drawls.

The Light from the West

Provincial. Where you dreaded a backwater
of antimacassared front parlours, flat hats, pigeon lofts,
Bingo with port and lemon on a Friday night,
I felt my feet rooted.

While you thought the capital the centre of the known world,
I heard myself howling, lost for all time
in the hell that is the London underground.

You should have said hayseed or hick and had done with it.
Back then, your insult cut me to the quick. But now,
I embrace it.

SLOW

I didn't bother much with birds, the stars,
the Latin names of plants, was quite uncouth.
I lived in flats and hung around in bars.
I liked my music loud and raw. In truth,
I loved fast men and even faster cars.
I worked to play. All that was in my youth,
but now I'm more sedate with gentler habits,
I dream of potting sheds, Angora rabbits.

DOG TAG

I

The family crept through his territory,
expecting artillery or the sniper's single shot,
sarcasm, delivered with deadly accuracy.
Small children rattled him, anything noisy or messy:
God knows what he'd made of Gallipoli.
But he loved me and tabby cats with flagpole tails,
both drawn to his bony lap, though he spoke to us sternly
and often at length.

Dress uniforms and striped blazers hung like ghosts
in his wardrobe, and sometimes on him, at seventy
lean as he'd been at twenty-seven.
I remember him in traction, somewhere in Wales;
time-travelling too fast through the swinging sixties,
on a country lane he'd hit a wall.

On the ward he stroked a surprise goatee;
it gave him a rakish, academic air,
but stripped of collar and silk cravat,
his bones rose too close to the surface,
sparse white hair straggled his chest
beneath hospital pyjamas.

Polishing the tarnish of decades
from this thin disc of silver,
I picture it lying against his skin and wonder:

Did his body crawl with lice?
Did he feel the prickle of cold sweat on gooseflesh,
fear he'd never make it home to his bride to father family?
Did he sense death stalking him through the dry gullies
of a fly-blown peninsula? Or worse, in the thunder of war
did he think he'd bottle it and run, take a bullet in the back?

The Light from the West

Or did he just fear the futility of falling silently
to dysentery, heatstroke, frostbite,
a mudslide in the thaw?

If so, he never said.

II

Instead I remember pantomimes,
just the two of us, our treat.
Grandpa in greatcoat and fedora,
me, dolled in velvet hat and collar,
hands warm in fur muff or mittens,
pretending to be Russian spies
as we walked to enormous, glittering theatres
through magical, snowy city streets.

Because it always snowed in winter then
and these were the days of make-believe.

After the matinée, afternoon tea:
he seemed familiar to commissionaires,
red-faced beneath white whiskers
outside posh hotels where liveried footmen,
lizards moonlighting from Cinderella,
ushered us in with a flourish.
My feet, encased in patent leather,
barely touched the rink-like floors.
Waiters set down tiny sandwiches,
cream cakes the size and lightness of clouds.

But I never saw him eat,
imagined he lived on Cuban cigars,
crystal glasses of Ribena.

III

I was sad at first, soon didn't miss him much at all,
caught by novelty: kitten, change of school.
He took to the hills, misted over in the mind's eye,
but sometimes now I have him in my sights

when I watch old men in Panama hats
taking the sun in seaside towns,
or catch the aroma of a fat Havana
lingering in an empty room.

He became as mis-remembered
as the colours of plants no longer grown,
the names of people once encountered
in another country, long ago.

His sons gone, now I'm the last of him
and next in the firing line, striving to capture
the essence of a man who slides away from me
like mercury in a saucer.

On the metal tag no trace of sweat or DNA,
just what's there when they roll your carcass over –
name, rank, religion, number – no space left
for soldier, dandy, lover, father.

BLOOD MOON

I wake to the soft pop of shotgun fire
across the fields, the farmer taking rabbits,
breaking into dreams, birdsong before first light.
And remember, at this time of Blood Moon,
the stiffening hare left hanging upside-down
on our back door, a brace of pheasants,
plumage still glossy in the slant gold flare of sunset,
gifts from our neighbour, Jack – the crack shot,
the fox-hunting vet, the mink breeder –
and wonder at the paradox he could hold in his mind.

I hear his urgent rat-a-tat at 3.00 a.m.,
his wife in sudden labour, picture my mother
roused from sleep, grabbing her black bag from the hall,
hurrying next door where lights blazed till morning.
I recall her tired eyes at breakfast and a small girl
rushing round there after school, agog
to see Jack's newborn son.

I remember Mother's initials, satin-stitched
on the slippery lining of the stole he gave her,
and why she didn't swathe her shoulders
in its luxury of an evening, come October.

SILKWEED

Craning out
beyond the water's edge,

I plunge one arm into warm slime,
pull out dripping handfuls

of duckweed spangles,
watermint lianas. Silt clouds

and gas bubbles rise, release
a dark ooze – slow rot, sweet renewal.

I rake the pool's surface, go deeper,
a police diver dragging a lake,

disturbing loose green strands
of silkweed, filamentous

as the hair of someone gone under
in the night –

slipsliding through tines and fingers.
Then I remember

a cotton candy woman,
her hot sugar drum, the floss flying

to her wand. I dip and twist
my spindle in the pond,

wind in
the thickening skeins.

TIME

I remember the gloom of the tap room and his notice:
NO OVERALLS TO BE WORN IN THE LOUNGE
where the old landlord held court behind his horseshoe bar;
the jar of pickled eggs, crisps with those blue twists of salt –
the only food to be had.

I remember especially the chairs –
woodwormed carvers, some straight-backed diners
and a miscellany dragged indoors from his patio
in the days before mismatch was the look to go for,
before we all went gastro with the deep leather sofas smelling
of luxury,
the qualities strewn artfully on distressed console tables
for a more desirable clientele to peruse.

I remember the maraschino cherry stabbed into a warm
Cinzano,
the half of cider he strove to serve in a 'lady's' glass.
Because you are a lady, aren't you?

I remember his melancholy wife,
one pale blue eye always slightly drifting,
and the hole she left in the upstairs window –
her sewing basket having missed his head –
and the jagged glass on the street below next morning
after she'd called time on him.

DURBAN

The air feels tropical here in the kitchen,
my hands smell of the ocean, garlic and chilli.
Do you remember the last time we ate prawns piri-piri,
grease running down our chins, our mouths on fire,
still calling out for more?
We never tasted a colour so hot!

Freewheeling to the coast in the cool almost dawn,
shadows in the folds of the rich red land,
women of the foothills, maids and cleaners, begin their long
trek to work,
thin clothes flapping against grey skin, wraiths rising
from the smoke of cooking fires
in the not quite light. We'd driven all night

through the mountains, it was coming on autumn
a hard blue cast to the ocean, the unsafe-to-swim signs
the possible sharks, that sand-blown shack
down a truck-rutted track, its tin roof, the shallow metal bowls
of hot red oil, the flesh tender yet resistant to the bite,
the brittle, translucent shells.

I should have sent your diamonds, some explanation back.
Forgive me, I have this unreliable streak.
They say: *Don't ever look back.*
Pick up your pen if you do.

O'CONNELL STREET 1963

A bouncy flight from Blackpool across the Irish Sea –
carried my mother, her father, my father and me.
A photo, boxed, now in my loft, an academic gown,
the embroidered serpent twined with the rod of healing:
such light in her eyes rarely seen, hair newly auburned,
teased into ramshorns in the style of the Queen.
After the ceremony, alumni, families, fellows mingled,
took tea and cake or sipped champagne on College Green.
We basked in her afterglow all afternoon.

Was there a supper, celebrations later? I don't recall –
but woke at dawn, opened wide the hotel curtains.
A shepherd swung his crook from side to side to drive his flock,
a hundred strong. Along O'Connell Street they clattered on
towards the livestock market, the one-way-ticket boats.

COD

They'd been sleeping on the Grand Banks,
in the waters off Iceland, later the deep White Sea,
silently translating themselves
into bread for our table.

My father slips out in the cold pre-dawn –
oiled knit, old Gannex, Dutch – not Lancashire – clogs –
making for the treacherous market floor
to bid for his share of the catch.

He oversees the transformation.
Salt cod hang stiff and stinking in the icy sheds,
awaiting resurrection on a plate as *bacalhau*
somewhere in Lisbon, Luanda, Lourenço Marques …

I roll the names over and over on my tongue
just for the romance of it, not knowing where these places are.
He lives in dread of strikes, impoundment and blocked ports,
the precious fish going past even their long point
of preservation.

Disembodied voices in the night, delays on the line
and the pads beside our phone all scrawled –
such and such a vessel late departing Liverpool –
another arrived elsewhere, unloading now –
condition good, sometimes fair.

And every Christmas a crate of pineapples
washes up from the Azores.

FINISHING SCHOOL

A Portrait of the Artist as a Young Woman

A Lausanne café photograph
shows loons, a butterfly emblazoned

across my breast, John Lennon specs
a legal glass of wine

cig in hand, no doubt song in mouth
I supple and suave.

Cool? I'm straight from the fridge, Dad
if a little nervous

defying the camera and all comers
in the strange light of some new world

you can read it in the face, the pose
with the arrogance of Icarus, I'm destined for the sun.

Goodbye, school!
I shake your dust from my shoes.

Look out, world!
There's a genius emerging and she's coming to get you ...

LONG GRASS SUNDAYS

Melanie lies back in the long grass
behind the Fylde Farm School.
We must never call it 'borstal'.
The boy shoos me away with a freckled hand.
Get lost, kidda. Leave us alone.
I wander off through heat-hazed fields,
sit down beside a green pond, watch slow cows
chew their way through Sunday afternoon.
I would never tell – I am Melanie's alibi
as she is mine these summer holidays.
But I cannot read her flushed face, the bruises
ripening on her neck like blackberries
as we drag ourselves home through the lanes.

What did anyone do for Sunday kicks back then?
How did we survive the stifling drive in Sunday best
to visit relatives in cramped city flats,
with the smell of mothballs in airless rooms,
the small talk, the tinned salmon,
the Light Programme?

My father retreated to his attic workshop
where he absently fixed things with solder and pliers
before the Sunday roast that no one wanted in summer.
And me, fidgeting, getting through it fast as possible.
Who said you could get down from the table?
Where are you going? Nowhere.

And then the waiting in the empty square
for the puttering Sunday bus to a smoke, a mooch
on the beach where a toe in the water became a wade
then a floating-on-your-back dream in summer.
Where have you been? Nowhere.

The Light from the West

Last Sunday, on the way upstairs,
I paused to consider the fields out back,
for weeks unmown, wind-battered, flattened by rain.
Like biblical tares, mares' tails and ragwort have crept in,
the perimeter grass grown tall as a man.

THE DRAWER LESS OPENED

The manual for a long-defunct oven;
a cylinder of nozzles, bag missing, presumed lost;
an egg-timer with a four-minute warning's worth of sand;
a meat-hook, bought for the young hen pheasant
I didn't shoot in next door's garden one September dawn,

but devoured instead like a half-starved vixen;
a butcher's striped apron; six sachets of aspirin
for reviving all-night garage chrysanths; a napkin ring
of dull grey steel, brought back by my father in '39 –
Die Liebe Geht Durch Dem Magen picked out with a drill,
as if by some dentist, both hungry and love-sick.
Blue birthday candles with clean white wicks;
a knife sharpener, screaming in its box;
a souvenir spoon with the shield of Reykjavik
and a hygrometer to gauge moisture in the grain I hoard
in my vast and shiny mid-Western silos.

The Light from the West

ISLAND

I've abandoned the volleyball, turned my back
on stacked sunbeds, furled umbrellas,
the universal mongrels
mated like magnets beneath the pines.
Neons flicker on as the sun goes down.
Specula dance on darkening water.

Wading out through clear shallows,
over sand rippled by the tides of aeons,
the slither tracks of sea snakes, monsters,
I feel no pebble underfoot to pocket
as a talisman. And anyway, I have no pockets,
being as I am, half naked.

If I looked down, I'd see small brown fish,
shoaling in evening phosphorescence.
But I must feed my fetish image;
blinker the edge of vision,
with closed fingers frame that other
island's whale-calf silhouette; serene,
basking in the last pool of light.

You would think I was working a miracle
so far out in the bay, like walking on Galilee,
until the seabed shelves suddenly away
and I'm out of my depth,
swimming towards Marathonisi
as she recedes from me.

I turn from the setting sun.
Besides, the place is barren, without trees, water,
home only to lizards, a zillion sandflies,
the occasional scorpion.
I've been there before.

The Light from the West

But my eyes are my camera,
my body, a night storage heater.
I've burned this light on the retina,
and hold this heat in the blood,
for slow release in dank November.

MARGARETHE

In her raw-boned heyday she'd loom in doorways,
her shadow blotting out the sun – it always
did surprise me she could cast one at all.
She was a bully. I felt very small.
If youthful joy or laughter filled the air
she'd promptly quell it with a baleful glare
or stamp it out with clomping, plod-like feet.
Her wiry hair, once black, turned grey as sleet
on steely seas or lonely moorland graves,
then grew out long in stiff, white waves.
Her cold grey eyes would bulge and roll, pale-lashed.
Her downcurled mouth, a startling crimson gash,
cursed the world, the wrong in all she saw –
the very best of times had been the war.
Pails of water were hurled at cats who dared
to cross her garden, stalk her birds. She seldom shared
the warmth of women's friendship yet would batten
fast on gossip heard, then pour its poison
in the ear of any man who'd listen.
This pious fiend preferred the words of chit-chat magazines
to those of William Shakespeare or Saint James –
her taste for mawkish greetings cards I blame.
Yet she was hard enough to only move
herself to sign them 'from' and never 'love'.
She took grim pleasure in the wintry gloom
of mystery tours to pokey, off-peak rooms
she shared with other widows in dead resorts,
in down-at-heel, genteel hotels. Her retort,
the day I called to say I'd joined that set,
was malign as ever she could get –
So, now you'll find out just what it's like.
She had me, skewered, on her twisted spike.

The Light from the West

For a while she brightened, burden lightened.
There's no pockets in shrouds, no shops in heaven.
Tea bags lay there drying on her kitchen sill.
Thereafter things between us went downhill.

Margarethe was one of several names given to the Wicked Stepmother in versions of Cinderella.

GUTTERING

You insist on climbing up there. Still stubborn
though less agile than you once were.
You think it's your job – what men do.
I am more sure-footed than you
but must stay on the ground, hold the ladder steady.
It's what women do. But should you lean out too far
and fall, I cannot catch you.

Wind and birds have sown the seeds
of small high gardens in our gutters. It takes all day
to circle the house. Underneath, I seethe and mutter
as you scrape and hurl down handfuls
of wet moss and weeds; clods of sodden earth
landing all around me, on me. I love you
but today I feel murderous.

You demand the hose, like a surgeon barking
for instruments. Standing on the bottom rung
I snake it up to you. The gutters brim, cascade,
flood the grass till the drains begin to gurgle.
You descend, pink-cheeked, triumphant, a happy god.
I let go the ladder then mud-spattered, speechless,
stomp indoors.

FOR GEORGE

I hadn't seen him up close in a decade,
Mister George Melly, seducing a Saturday morning crowd in
Boots –
perhaps he'd just dived in for aspirin, linctus –
comfortably louche in his slouch hat and mad plaid suit.
And the counter girls and I and all of us
were clapping Good Time George, his voice
rich and mellow as fruit cake
soaked in vintage brandy.

He was already getting on. And incidentally,
just warming his throat for a lunchtime gig next door.

When I got back to the car you didn't believe me!
So I sulked and stomped and grooved and blued and hollered.
All day. Inside my head. Also, other bits of me.

After that, whenever we watched him on the telly,
extemporising on The Big Stuff – you know,
Music, Sex, Fishing, Art and Life – I'd remind you
he'd been right there in Boots, Knutsford, that one Saturday,
The Man, Melly. And you'd missed him!
Raising your eyes to heaven, you'd shake your head.
Why do you persist in this fantasy?

I never knew him – yet loved him.
And sleepless, last night at 3.30, watching again
that final documentary charting his slow, defiant fade,
I got up from my bed, put my favourite album on
and laughed, ragged around the kitchen till dawn.

PINK

Silence the echoes of Barbara Cartland;
shocking pink lipstick and daddy's little darlings
in Tesco tiaras and Princess pink dresses;
ban candyfloss; bubble-gum; day-glo petunias;
hot-house tulips; gaudy new dahlias;
all foods and fabrics dyed with cochineal,
pulverised shells of innocent beetles.

Rejoice in the expectation of cherubim
lounging on clouds above dusky pink cities;
the tongues of all felines; the palest of strawberry fools;
sugared almonds; damask roses, blowsy and sweet;
old Persian carpets in sun-faded drawing rooms.
A certain crushed velvet ball gown
that was mine at twenty-one.

ROLLMOPS

I remember his hands
when I think of them at all
as small for a big man
see them red, calloused
smell them redolent of brine
feel them almost always warm.

He's back in the old kitchen
filleting herrings for rollmops –
onions, dill, sea-salt, peppercorns,
wooden toothpicks, vinegar on the side.
Heads/tails/fins fall away
in a flash of steel, little backbones
flicked out in one.

Imagining the battlements at Elsinore,
the spy-ridden place,
the whiff of something rotten, I ask:

Did you find the place? What was it like?
And show me the backbone trick with the fish.

He turns to me, I find his eyes
grey-blue fathomless,
with that curious cold opacity
of the Øresund.

Yes, I found the place. A small port.
I told you a hundred times –
not much more than a fishing village.
It rained a lot. And I did show you. Often.
But you were never watching.

HUMOUR

ONE NIGHT AN IRIS

One night an iris
without warning began to grow
out of the top of my head.

I took pleasure in its deep green fronds
and, when they came, the sky-blue flowers,
in their throats licks of flame;
the way heads turned when I stepped into a room,
a chorus girl high-kicking out of line,
my head-dress of blooms and foliage
where ostrich feathers might have swayed.

Soft summer petals furled and died.
Stems could not hold the weight
of seed pods that swelled and split,
spitting hard red beads like shot
to ricochet about my feet.

There was no point, I reasoned –
the onslaught of autumn, no birds flying –
in pruning shears or secateurs, seeing clearly
that the problem lay rooted deep inside my skull.
Four-square before the bathroom mirror
I steeled myself, first took up trowel then scalpel
to excavate the alien rhizome.

The Light from the West

IN WHICH I, ARTURO, AM LIKENED TO AN ARTICHOKE

We lived in peace until the peacocks came,
strutting and screaming in his garden. And at first
there was just the one cabinet, not large but exquisite:
though still an extravagance, as I remarked at the time.
A cornucopia of jewelled reliquaries, wantonings of Nature,
bezoars that sweat in the presence of poison.

So I indulged him, judging it a passing fancy.
But that was only the start of it.
Classify everything that arrives, Arturo, he says.
Put like with like, bone with tusk, malachite with figured stone,
skeletons of seahorse beside chameleon.
But, I ask, are gilded ostrich eggs Art or Nature?
Is the winged cat bird or beast?
These days he buys more than he sells.
And guess who shoulders the burden?
I, Arturo, his loyal major-domo.

He instructs me to respect the natural order of things;
that the kitchen servants are tubers and root vegetables.
He, of course, is a rare fruit – quince or pomegranate.
But you, he said, Arturo, are an artichoke.
Why? Because you have a tender heart.
He thinks this the best joke ever made,
slaps his thighs and laughs till he cries.

This is my favourite piece, our Janissary ape,
wrought by an artificer in Constantinople.
See how the great arms move so smoothly,
almost like a man's, as he lifts the pitiless mirror.
Observe the discomfiture of our visitors,
twitching as they adjust their dress,
unsure how to conduct themselves
in the sight of such wonders.

The Light from the West

Now look out into the garden beyond this chamber,
at the troupe of chattering monkeys,
the solitary dromedary and the vicious spotted cat.
Which I am minded to release.
To silence the accursèd peacock screams.

The Light from the West

HEIGH HO, SILVER

The purple sage is burning black,
a twister hoovered up our shack –
and it ain't exactly comin' back –
then the mail train slid clean off the track.
Oh my! Calamity! Heigh ho, Silver.
We're leavin' Arizona.

Well, Pa got high on cactus juice,
produced a deck without a deuce –
he's ridin' shot on Joe's caboose –
he's better off out on the loose.
Oh my! Calamity! Heigh ho, Silver.
We're leavin' Arizona.

My puppy dawg got sick and died –
that vetinary, how he lied!
And I got a notion, deep inside
them green tomatoes ain't been fried.
Oh my! Calamity! Heigh ho, Silver.
We're leavin' Arizona.

Grandma's crashed my pick-up truck,
I'm stuck in Hicksville without a buck –
ain't never felt so out of luck –
and Ol' Grampy, he don't give a …
Oh my! Calamity! Heigh ho, Silver.
We're leavin' Arizona.

Dangerous Jake gone stole my horse,
Great Aunt Louella's on the sauce,
my Jethro wants a quick divorce
but dang, I love him still, of course.
Oh my! Calamity! Heigh ho, Silver.
We're leavin' Arizona.

The Light from the West

No place to lay my hat, my head,
no rhinestone cowboy in my bed –
some low-rent cheapskate punk instead.
I had to fill him full of lead.
Oh my! Calamity! Heigh ho, Silver.
We're leavin' Arizona.

The eagle's bald, the crops done failed
and I cain't sing like Crystal Gayle.
The Devil's posse's on my trail,
I'll end up in the County Jail.
Oh my! Calamity! Heigh ho, Silver.
We're leavin' Arizona.

The sarsasparilla mine's caved in,
mad coyotes roam the caverns.
Ma's run off with the preacher man,
bar-keep's barred me from the tavern.
Oh my! Calamity! Heigh ho, Silver
We're leavin' Arizona.

Though the river's dry at Cripple Creek
my blue suede shoes still sprung a leak,
Alice Cooper called me an effin' freak –
so the outlook's lookin' pretty bleak.
Oh my! Calamity! Heigh ho, Silver.
We're leavin' Arizona.

My lasso's frayed, my blades are wrecked,
can't hang myself, can't slit my neck.
Life's a bitch but what the heck?
Ain't waitin' for that welfare check.
Oh my! Calamity! Heigh ho, Silver.
We're leavin' Arizona.

The Light from the West

The Yankees call us trailer trash
but I think we're cuttin' quite a dash –
a little Crosby, Stills and Nash –
you'll catch me down at Country Splash.
Oh my! Calamity! Heigh ho, Silver.
We're leavin' Arizona.

HARAJUKU LOVERS

My Harajuku Lovers
have hearts of black enamel
badged beneath the arches
where veins rise like rivers.
Their red lacquered heels
click-clack on the pavement,
please me when I walk.

Oriental hip-hop girls
all crop tops and baseball caps
break-dance in comic strip
across my printed soles.
Their dreadlocks bounce,
they pose and pout, staring out
through widened, Western eyes.

But these are no 'fuck me' shoes.
These shoes are Art with a capital A,
an internet thunderbolt,
bought untouched, untried,
the female's heart always younger
than her feet – my feet, now bound
by cruel pink stitching.
How I suffer for their beauty,
their pinching peacock uppers.

Hidden by the freesheet on the Metro,
sashimi-ed in between commuters,
my knees crossed, an ankle flexed,
tiny peep-toes pointing out
the valise rack overhead,
I listen to the jealous whispers
about my Harajuku Lovers.

HISTORY

ON SHAKESPEARE'S 450TH BIRTHDAY

You've shown us love gone bad, betrayal, madness:
we're your schemers, dreamers, driven creatures.

You speak to Everyman and for all time –
a realm that spans the gutter and the gods.

You'd feel at home in Liverpool this spring –
a reborn theatre staging one of yours.

Come back to weave the threads of soaps and sitcoms,
post your playwright's blog online each day,
go spinning through our virtual, wicked world.

Yes, we know all about your dodgy friends.
And we don't mind. We keep a few ourselves.

But tell us why she had to have at last
your second-best – a gift that still annoys –
and why your female roles were played by boys.

'second-best' refers to the bed WS is said to have bequeathed to his wife, Anne Hathaway

TZARINA

I tell you there are matchless diamonds sewn
into the hems of my daughters' dresses against the night
when the roaring horsemen will come

like thunder over the mountains. Meanwhile men spit
on my face on their roubles. I find roses of blood
in bloom under my son's skin. All day the guards are stupid

with vodka – in our grey tea the taste of ashes. I kneel before God
as the boy shivers, lacking the charcoal to keep the samovar
warm. And all the food they'll give us is stale black bread.

I'm a woman. I hanker after trinkets. But my little silver
jam spoons vanished with our ikons. Like alchemic architects
the comrades change the merchant's jewel-box villa

into a mausoleum for us, an outlandish gilded casket.
All night their sentries sleepwalk through the basement.

RUSSIAN CARAVAN

Yes, I regret the Baltic amber
we brought so far to please them
but the jade, the painted porcelain
they gave us in return ~
pouches of ginger, bamboo boxes ~
I would have ditched the lot
unhitched it in the mountains in the snow.

Through whiteouts on the taiga
we wore aromatic caches, close to our skin
kept cloves always in our mouths, chewed them
to soothe the screaming cold-borne toothache
that swelled our wind-flayed faces.
Men howled like wolves, mad with pain.

In Siberia we remembered
mulberry orchards, moon gates,
summer's languor in the hidden world behind the Wall.
And camels, frisky from the grasslands
carrying us swiftly under a curved desert sky
indigo folds in the distant Altai mountains
our first sight of Baikal's bottomless turquoise
rags fluttering in the birches like long white messages
dancing shamans, the clear-eyed craziness of the Old Believers.

Later, we cursed our loose-wheeled carts, our packhorse sleds
the drawn-out exchanges on the border
the impossible bull hides, the wretched leaves, the threat of
mould ~
all bought with Russian furs and gold.
So we cursed the musquash, ermine, silver fox and sable
all panners and miners, their filthy yellow metal.

The Light from the West

But still the endless land floated, on and on
insubstantial before us ~ the needle spinning, the lodestone useless.
Sane men went raving alone into the wilderness.

Then sudden lights hung in the frozen air ~
a boom town nestling in the dark flanks of a valley.
They beckoned, glinting like a jewelled garter on a young
widow's thigh.
So we entered the makeshift town, some limping, some swaggering ~
the tea pioneers of the wild Far East.

Well, the whores teased us, fussed us, plied us with rotgut
then left us without a rouble face down in the ice
outside the walls of the merchants' gimcrack villas
while horsemen haggled over muskets in the market stalls.

The Light from the West

MARY MILLER

*From the Genesee Hotel Suicide photograph by local press photographer,
I. Russell Sorgi
Buffalo, NY, 8 May 1942. Witness statement/extract from* Life
magazine

It's Friday, kind of blowsy, nothing much doing,
and I'm driving through the warm homeward afternoon –
no plans for the weekend – a little cheesed perhaps because of this.
And that. Then this voice inside my head starts nagging me,
butting in:
Sorgi, can't you even do one damn thing to change your life?
Take a different route or something for God's sake?
So I make a random turn and suddenly everything changes:
I'm following a cop car speeding down Main,
sirens wailing, the whole shebang.
They stop outside the Genesee Hotel –
there's a crowd gathered and I park anywhere I can,
note all the upturned faces, eyes shielded against the sun,
in grimy windows reflections of the buildings over,
the lady officer talking with the doorman.
The blond perches on an eighth-floor ledge,
swinging her legs, waving at the crowd below.
Someone says she's been there twenty minutes
and if she meant it, she'd have done it by now.

I snatch the camera from the car,
squeeze out two quick shots of her, then take my chance,
figure I'll reload the holder, get set for another …
She waves again, clutching the air vent,
then pushes herself off into space.
The action goes slo-mo as she travels:
I take a firm grip on myself, wait till she's passing
the third, no, second storey, depress the shutter

The Light from the West

just as she reaches the mezzanine,
where the guys in the coffee shop looking out
have no idea what's coming down.
Boy, you could see everything. And I mean
everything.

But I guess she's past caring.

I held my cool and caught her mid-fall,
a fairy doll flying out on a wire.
The rubbernecks screamed, then went quiet.
Did I do wrong? I could do nothing to save her.
And sometimes folk need a change from war.

THE BALLAD OF 'LUCKY' TOWER

Show me a man without a dream
and I'll show you a half-dead fool.
That's why I crossed the Irish Sea
and came to Liverpool.

At anchor lay a fine corvette
so I took the silver shilling.
But one dark night I stole away.
You could say I was unwilling.

William Clark slips out of sight
and in steps Francis Toner;
my fate to roam the seven seas
from Perth to Barcelona.

I rattled round from port to port
and soon fetched up in Durban.
I fought the Boer down the years
then shipped once more as fireman.

The blast from the boiler threw me clear
when the iceberg gashed *Titanic*.
She went straight down like a babe to sleep
to her grave in the cold Atlantic.

William Clark slips out of sight
and in steps Francis Toner
in sharp cut suit and Yankee boots.
Who wants to sail with a Jonah?

A Canada liner out of The Pool
with her hold full of mail and silver;
at Quebec the cat refused to board.
Lord, how we tried to coax her.

The Light from the West

But the Star of the Sea protected me
on the foggy St Lawrence River.
One thousand souls were lost that night
as the *Empress* rolled hard over.

The torpedo struck so I ran on deck
and jumped from the *Lusitania*.
She sank like a stone off Kinsale Old Head.
Friend, don't let me detain ya.

Some folk say I've a charmed feckin' life
and some folk say that I'm lying.
Why should I care? I cheated Death.
One more, sir, cheers, if you're buying.

William Clark slips out of sight
and in steps Francis Toner
in sharp-cut suit and Yankee boots.
Who wants to sail with a Jonah?

So cometh the hour then cometh the man
but the sea holds all the power.
A printer's error changed my name,
now they call me 'Lucky' Tower.

ISLE OF THE CROSS

When drought parched the gardens of Hawarden
and crops lay dying in the fields,
the Hardeners, facing the spectre of famine,
went down on their knees to pray to the Virgin.
The most pious of these, the wife of the Governor,
would beg and beseech Her, pester and test Her
till the statue grew angry and stilled her.
It toppled and crushed her and killed her
at Hawarden, west of the city of Chester.

In turn the people of Hawarden grew angry
and tried the Virgin for the death of the lady,
finding Her guilty of murder
and failing to answer their prayers.

They couldn't forgive Her but baulked at the gallows,
fearing their souls would be damned,
so they laid the Virgin down in the shallows
by the banks of the River Dee.
Then the tide rushed in and swept Her
up to the walls of Chester and drowned Her
where the people found Her and blessed Her
and buried Her statue beneath a cross, saying:
She has come to us – it is Hawarden's loss.
They mocked the Hardeners and put them to shame
till the river rose and a deep flood came
and only the cross on its mound could be seen.

Now racehorses gallop round and round
on grass that grows on solid ground
at The Roodee down by the river,
outside the city walls of Chester.

The Light from the West

Note from author

The name Roodee means Isle of the Cross and these lines (which I didn't want to include in the poem) were said to have been inscribed on the cross, now lost:

The Jews their God did crucify
The Hardeners theirs did drown:
Because their wants she'd not supply
And she lies under this cold stone.

From *The Fabled Coast* by Sophia Kingshill and Jennifer Westwood

THE SHADOW FLYERS

Once more sentries were posted from the heights
to where pines reach down to the water's edge.
Again the men spread out, hid in the pigeon's terrain
above that beach where oyster-catchers feed.
These watchers doused all fires and bore no lights.
They did not speak or hum or stamp their feet
though this night was cold, the pale moon
a winter-settled bride, veiled in mist.
They neither saw nor heard the ship of death
as it stole upriver, gliding swiftly towards our shore,
oars feathering on the incoming tide,
silent as owl wings ghostly beating.
Perceiving no breath, no peturbation of the night, no threat,
our kinsmen bivouacked beneath a cloak of bracken,
scent of herb and resin crushed underfoot,
lulling our warriors into dreamless sleep.
Thus the sly marauders crept upon us with the dawn,
sword in hand, slaughter uppermost in their hearts.

JOURNEY OF THE PILGRIMS

(after T.S. Eliot)

A warm coming we had of it
in the dying of the year,
an overnight hop on that tub of a ship,
the bars full and the cabin squalid,
the very height of naff.
And the stewards bored, the passengers lairy,
our passports unstamped on an unrecorded journey.
There were times we regretted the Cypriot tavernas,
and the poolside jocks bringing cocktails.
Then our driver, stretching at dawn, revealing
the blue tattooed number on the inside of his forearm,
and the engine running hot all the way to Jerusalem,
the girl soldiers with machine guns, flirting and chewing gum.
And the guide weaseling away our awkward questions,
the sweep of millennia in one whistle-stop morning:
The Temple Mount and the site of Golgotha,
and Al-Aqsa, off limits but so close you could touch it.
In the end we preferred to sneak away,
slipping down back alleys, with his voice
ringing in our ears, saying
this land is all holy.

Then at lunchtime we came into Bethlehem –
a hot, white town, smelling of sweat and cardamom,
with motorbikes and fruit stalls and joyful pilgrims.
An old man whittled cradles and crosses out of olive wood.
On Manger Square I searched inside myself, inside the church,
for some rekindling. Kneeling on the cold stone floor,
I kissed the Star, feeling nothing, but the patina of centuries,
the hope of millions.

The Light from the West

All this was long ago,
before so many mortars, so many martyrs,
before Checkpoint 300,
before the Wall of Separation. I remember
and I would not do it again, but wonder:

Do we explore the origins of the universe,
and walk in space, a fragile people,
still clutching our gods for this?

Peace be with you, Salaam Aleikum, Shalom.

1000 LASHES

On the sentencing of the Saudi blogger, Raif Badawi, to 1000 lashes to be carried out 50 lashes at a time.

Raif, they have you cornered like a mouse
in a room without a door. They pounce.
They bat you slowly, paw to paw,
then bide their time until their 'doctors' give the clear
to lacerate and flay your body raw.

They came for you, brother, as they will come
for all the others who dare to walk against the crowd.
And we who walk between two worlds
compromise ourselves to make the most of both.
We hold our noses, fool ourselves with weasel words:
My enemy's enemy must be my friend.

We avert our eyes from your welted, bloodied flesh,
we stop our ears and *la-la-la* out loud
so we cannot hear you scream. But lash by lash,
we flinch and find ourselves
screaming with you.

NATURE

SPRAWL

Man would have nature at his beck and call
with disciplined borders and a barbered verge,
but a woman likes a garden given to sprawl.

If her jasmine dare overspill his wall,
he'll snip at the tendrils in a muttering scourge.
Man would have nature at his beck and call,

cull the rampant, the bushy, the tall,
the gaudy, the shady, the unplanned splurge.
But a woman likes a garden given to sprawl.

He'll sweep away petals as fast as they fall,
poison each weedling in a vengeful purge.
Man would have nature at his beck and call.

She inhabits the seasons, her body in thrall
to wilt and dieback then burgeon and surge,
and a woman is a garden given to sprawl.

If foxgloves bloom, she'll cut some for the hall,
watch rank wildness and artifice merge.
Man would have nature at his beck and call;
woman, like a garden, is given to sprawl.

WAITING FOR RAIN

Sometimes before a storm, inside my skull
I feel my brain shrivel, a single seed
rattling in a dry pod, ready to split and spill.
Moving through the days, I live only in the physical,
absently pulling weeds from loose baked soil,
cleaning rooms, shopping like an automaton.

Sick of bad dreams, their half-remembered visions,
of waking jittery in the not quite light,
tearful, on the brink, the sky about to fall.
I want to disappear, hide in long grass
while dust and blown petals spiral on sudden gusts,
gather in the margins of my mind.

Skin, hair sparking static, eyes red and gritty,
my body sweaty, hyper-sensitive to charged particles
jostling in saturated air, the low pressing down on me,
mercury falling as dew point gets closer.
I long for the purge of a deluge.

With the first drops peace comes back to me.
Squalls batter on glass, then in full spate
rain bounces off concrete, the gutters can't cope.
And when it's over, the air sweet again,
all that weight lifted, floating in the clearest light,
I begin to notice a greening of the mind,
the heart replenished, the world brought round.

PANTOUM FOR AUTUMN

Come November, when thoughts turn to leaves,
harvest over, the house martins long flown south –
the tired and silent land waits for fog and mist
to roll and fold the earth in sleep.

Harvest over, the house martins long flown south,
days shrink, and cold black nights steal in
to roll and fold the earth in sleep.
It's so still you almost forget to breathe.

Days shrink and cold black nights steal in.
How to survive the coming winter?
It's so still you almost forget to breathe
but for the catch and tang of wood-smoke on the air.

How to survive the coming winter?
Kick through russet drifts. Watch geese fly in chevron.
But for the catch and tang of wood-smoke on the air
you might spin alone in your own dark space.

Kick through russet drifts. Watch geese fly in chevron
as the vivid world bleeds colour.
You might spin alone in your own dark space,
weave a shroud of moss and lichen.

As the vivid world bleeds colour
the tired and silent land waits for fog and mist.
Patch a quilt of puce and crimson
come November when thoughts turn to leaves.

LOTUS EATING

Don't take me out walking in Owley Wood
when fog shrouds those towering conifers.
Don't try to shift me from my own fireside
while I nurse my winter melancholia.
Wait until spring, when suburban cats laze
mid-stroll, stretch and roll on sun-warmed pavements
and I can't help but scan the skies
for early swifts, scouting to claim old haunts
beneath my eaves. Then lead me by the hand
through a deep green maze, an hour after sundown,
the air bat-filled and balmy, as our friends
in the south feel the first chills of autumn.
Let's loaf this precious time away, lotus eating.
Winter is long, summer all too fleeting.

STARLINGS

May

Jaded from night flight,
I turn my key. The air inside tastes
more than two weeks trapped.
The housecats sulk, blank me from the stairs,
it will take days to woo them back.
Pipes judder, the tap spews fetid water,
I grab my bathrobe, climb the ladder,
clamber from joist to joist, note the tell-tale
split of sky between rafters; the cupped nest
of down and grasses, half hidden by lumber;
the loft, spattered with shit and feathers,
and curse myself for the tank's ill-fitting lid,
pity the drowned bird in her panic.
But the young have fledged.

January

Iridescent in sunlight,
as if they passed through a prism or a slick
of petrol, the spike-feathered punks of the air
bicker and jostle round the feeder.
On some secret signal or a cue from Hitchcock,
flocks begin to gather, starlings without number
crowding high in bare oaks, massing
on the wires like crotchets on a stave.
The din of a tuning orchestra fills the afternoon,
then a sudden hush, a hold-your-breath tension
and I wait for an unseen maestro
to raise his baton, release
headlong glissandos of birds
into the deepening blue.

COMMON WEEDS CUT-UP

(Template Poem after Elma Mitchell)

Milk-thistle, lamb suckling,
baby's tears, mother's heart.

Blinks, chick-wittles,
downy woundwort, knitbone.

Flirt-wort. Touch-me-not,
ladies' fingers, milkmaids.

Loosestrife, beggary.
Old-man-in-the-spring.

Crowfoot. Cough-wort.
Deaf nettle, feverfew, piss-a-bed.
Staggerweed, quack grass.

Bitter nightshade.
Red archangel.
Death-come-quickly.

Black bindweed,
dead man's bells,
earth smoke.

Yorkshire fog.

PUFFBALL ROULETTE

It does not shriek like mandragora
as I lift its parchment stalk from beneath the oak
but begins instead to weep milk tears –
its head snapped off so carelessly.

Tawny cap, bell tutu fading into peach:
Penny Bun or Sulphur Tuft?

I flip it over on its underside, touch
its feathered petticoat; its underskirt, ruched;
the delicate pallor of its bloodless gills.

Nosing it, I expect the smell of rich damp earth,
of labyrinthine networks branching underground.
But detect only faint disappointment.

Those Russians out foraging in weekend woods
know which to take and which to leave.
This could be goblin fruit – corrupting and corrupt.

Do not slice and sprinkle with herbs
to fold into a chancy omelette.
Wash hands before touching mouth.

PROTEA

I am Protea. Once I ran wild beside a river
in Africa. I was outrageous cochineal.
I was green. I was silver. In December
I was uprooted from my warm red soil,
sold into sunless exile in another hemisphere.
But she said I was natural, magical,
more tasteful than tinsel, more subtle

than mistletoe, then stuck me alone
in a tall glass vase on a cold window sill.
In February my leaves fell. She took secateurs,
severed my stem then she left me to desiccate
and vegetate in her gun-metal fruit-bowl.
In April I'm still beautiful as a pale sea anemone,
a pink artichoke, or a husky pineapple from the Azores

but I languish among the papery orange lanterns
of the seven Chinese gooseberries waiting to garnish
a posh pudding she knows will never happen,
plus six cellulite lemons, two shrivel-skinned pippins
and one William pear deliquescing to mush.
A bevy of purple plums arrived today, luscious
and juicy, all sheen and bloom but I told them

Get out if you can while the going's good –
the only hope for you here is to get stewed.

A PACT

Through early morning rain-streaked glass,
I notice a drift of down on the lawn,
rafts of moss turned emerald in the night,
and think of rings and bones and earthworms
rising up through waterlogged land,
see the corpse behind the oak:
a woodpigeon, splayed, grey wings broken,
like a Hercules downed before dawn.

Later. I say. *I'll fetch the spade. After the rain.*

But the corvids come,
still scavenging in the storm.
The lone magpie, heretic bird of The Ark,
(chattering *chacker, chacker* as the world drowns),
pecks the first wound in the side of the neck
as the carrion crow swoops, cawing, down.
They flap and fight for the rain-soaked feast,
then settle to strip the flesh from the bones,
leaving enough for the fox to take in the night,
a drift of down on the lawn
next morning.

CONMAN AUTUMN

At first you barely notice him sliding
one foot under the back door frame.
Sighing softly, insinuating himself as he displays
swatches of the season's must-have colours.
You can still remember bright blue days
spent kicking through crisp leaves with a lover,
the rhythmic pull of the academic year, your taste
for strong meat after summer's vapid picnic.

Then you feel the crick in the back of the neck,
fear structural damage. Early darkness holds no intimacy now.
Autumn: time of obscuring mists, worm casts, toadstools,
piles of sodden leaves. Let the gales scatter them.
Bow-legged crone, put down your futile broom.
Jack-knife yourself indoors for a dish of soup.

FOR ST ELMO

Deflector of electric shock,
see to the upkeep of lightning conductors,
the safety of masons restoring gargoyles
high on cathedral spires.
You who were given a coat of molten metal,
intercede for the lead thieves.
Preserve them from sudden gusts, loose tiles and worn soles.
Hold scaffolders and steeplejacks in the palm of your hand.
Companion of seagulls, guard the sailors of tall ships,
keep your dancing fire from their mastheads,
the jibs and sheaves of cranes and oil rigs.
Counsel the bridge builders and the would-be
jumpers from bridges, all those seduced by thoughts
of one last flight into the beautiful void.
Bring them back from the ledge.
Walk beside the children of Blondin, the charmed lifers,
trapeze artistes and sky walkers
inching between towers of steel, the human flies
who cling to walls of glass.
Banish vertigo and blackouts.
Do not let them plunge.
Guide the linesmen and transmitter engineers,
all those who edge along girders and gantries,
spanning domes and theatres.
Martyr, snatched by an angel from a pit of vipers,
catch the falling. You who were nurtured
by ravens in the mountains, lift the hearts
of winchmen, rescue the rescuers,
and teach us to look up.

COME NOVEMBER

Come November, when thoughts turn to leaves,
harvest over, the swallows long flown south –
the tired and silent land waits for fog and mist
to roll and fold the earth in sleep.

Harvest over, the swallows long flown south,
days shrink and cold black nights steal in
to roll and fold the earth in sleep.
So still you almost forget to breathe.

Days shrink and cold black nights steal in.
How to survive the coming winter?
So still you almost forget to breathe
but for the catch and tang of wood-smoke on the air.

How to survive the coming winter?
Kick through russet drifts. Watch geese fly in chevron.
But for the catch and tang of wood-smoke on the air
you might spin alone in your own dark space.

Kick through russet drifts. Watch geese fly in chevron
as the vivid world bleeds colour.
You might spin alone in your own dark space,
weave a shroud of moss and lichen.

As the vivid world bleeds colour
the tired and silent land waits for fog and mist.
Patch a quilt of puce and crimson
come November, when thoughts turn to leaves.

WINTER SLEEPWALKING

In the softness of the old year's turning
he visited my garden, feasted on split nuts and bacon rind
three days together, the hawfinch with his blush-pink breast.
So I came to expect him, regard him as my own good omen.
Now there's snow in the forecast, a ring around the moon,
low sun brightens grudgingly like an eco-friendly lamp.
And I am bereft of the bird.

I see my breath hanging in the freezing air
when I haul in a scuttleful and logs for the fire.
Skeletal trees loom through muffling fog
and cat-ice skins the black pond.
Nothing smells or sounds of anything anymore.
I wait to be wakened from winter sleepwalking
by the green detonations of spring.

ART

RIVER IRWELL TIME

(Bailey Bridge, Manchester 1912 by Adolphe Valette)

One horizontal ties the verticals
as a line of mill stacks recedes upriver
into Manchester's acid murk and drizzle.

It's late afternoon, a winter nightfall.
His palette holds charcoal, turquoise, eau de Nil,

he's steeped his canvas in a solution of verdigris
scraped off old copper coins. Peer deep into the wet mist,
you'll catch the bargees' muffled calls, the thrash of fish

drowning in the Irwell – last gasps of a river trade
strangled by canal and rail.

A small boat waiting in the shadows
shows a dot of lantern light – its long-tailed reflection
surprising as a Spanish exclamation.

But Valette, loving this city, let its pea soup fogs,
its soft relentless rain seep under his skin, into his soul.

Now the digital photographer searches for the holes
left behind by the artist's easel, sets his tripod down
to merge the industrial past with a burnished steel future.

As loft people travel pixel by pixel across the time span,
fish are returning to this reach of the river.

JAZZ

What I like about jazz
Is how it makes you move those shoulders, hips, feet

What I like about feet
Is their high or even fallen arches

What I like about arches
Is the sound of voices bouncing off brickwork

What I like about brickwork
Is its roughness

What I like about roughness
Is the rasp of cats' tongues

What I like about cats' tongues
Is their pink satisfaction

What I like about satisfaction
Is measured in cigarettes

What I like about cigarettes
Is the way smoke rings deliver messages

What I like about messages
Is openness to interpretation

What I like about interpretation
Is a definition of jazz

INTROSPECTION

SOMETHING OF THE NIGHT

Early doors as daylight fades behind tall trees,
swifts dart and dive in silhouette, swoop
to nests beneath ancient eaves.
Midges seethe in molecular clouds,
fantails quieten in the dove-cote.

Dusk is not the hour between dog and wolf
but the hour between bird and bat.
Lights come on inside the bar,
bugs flit and shimmy around our candle.
Now, without doubt, night has fallen.

Later I walk in my moon-bleached garden,
the hum of night-freight on the soft, still air.
Across shadowed fields the town glows red,
a jewelled quilt spread out for pilots
on this floating bed of land.

I put out the light but the mind grinds on,
every shift and sigh of the house amplified by the dark.
With every bark and hoot and call and cry, I try
to remember love, find myself again

in the staff canteen,

a party going on. I wear a fairy costume
but carry a cartoon bomb labelled BOMB!!!
It is heavy as a bowling ball. I send it spinning
a slow-mo arc across the room. WHOOSH!
The city is a roaring pit of flame.

The Light from the West

I snap awake, rigid, gasping. The wind lifts
open curtains, shapes take on three dimensions,
a long mirror, a chair draped in last night's clothes.
There are cloud formations, the beginnings of light.
Birdsong.

A young fox, all yellow brush and nerve
drinks from the pond before padding home,
wood-pigeons lumber across the lawn.

The day shift is clocking on.

The Light from the West

MESSAGE FROM MCNAUGHT

As a night diver homes to the lamp
that burns on deck, I break the surface of sleep,
jar awake in the wreck of the bed.
Jangled. Mardy. Out of joint.

In the digital glow before dawn, my radio mutters on.
Piracy. Murder. State-run torture.

In the darkness of the landing window, a new star
bright as the full moon at perihelion,
travels fast and low across the paling sky,
long tail trailing in the solar wind
like a widow's uncut mane of grief,
unlucky as a stone thrown; a sailor
crowned with fire.

The secret code, lost blueprint of our lives
could be held, it's said,
in this nomad sphere of ice and dust,
hurtling out of the Oort Cloud.
Which may or may not exist.

McNaught powers out of Leo,
past Corvus and on towards Altair
making for the sun.
A yellow fox pads across frosted grass,
stares up at me and I understand.
Nothing.

NO LULLABY

But for the fox's bark; screech of owl;
the spit, hiss, yowl of caterwaul;
the creaking surrender of the house as it falls
into the black hole of night; the drumbeat
of my own heart, sometimes out here
things get too quiet for sleep.
These sounds sing no lullaby to me.

Then I want a gale – wild, bad-ass weather:
rain streaming over gutters, the lash
of branches against my window.
But I drift off to radio, rise to birdsong
above the low rumble of freight on the rat-run,
reps on the road early to feed the motorway hum
building between the North and Brum.

Then I miss the noise of the city:
the disembodied voices of station announcers;
the purr of black cabs, idling, turning;
the drivers' wound-down-window banter;
the cacophony from the gyratory;
the murmured snatches of conversation
in languages I don't understand.

I miss the lost boom of foghorns on the river;
the East–West tristesse of Roma buskers.
As the key slides from major to minor
their wailing brass breaks me down
like a witness to a stand-off in a Balkan fastness,
the cleaving of the age-old faultline
where we all guess the outcome.

JUBILO

You pilot me
through the shoals of night, lull me
when the shipping forecast can't.
You quiet the idiot who rambles through my mind
mithering as if she owned the place
even though she doesn't.
And you know so much!
You go anywhere, everywhere,
yet you always take me with you.
As the western world turns from moonlight
to face the sun, I listen, learn.
You make me get political!
Your phone-ins are phenomenal!
You introduce me to exceptional people.
You startle me with rumblings from far-away countries,
views from villages, cities I can only imagine.
You transport me to sinister installations in Kazakhstan,
African bush schools, sweatshops in Bangladesh.
You expand my consciousness
with music from desert places.
It stays with me all day.
How badly I need your updates!
Because mostly I don't know what goes on
the other end of our street. Lately, I've taken
to skimming the papers, often miss the news on TV,
preferring blues or silence.
But I trust you to tell the truth, unslanted;
not manipulate my thoughts – unlike some I could mention.
You have the power to stop me moving through this world
as if I lived at the centre of the universe, careless,
knowing nothing of how it goes elsewhere.
You are a community – exiles, friends and strangers.
You are a lone voice – intimate in the darkness,
speaking to me only, through my headphones.

The Light from the West

At 05.30, the night shift over, I try to picture you
setting yours aside, leaving the studio,
walking quickly down the Strand,
faceless in the early morning rain.

THE DIVIDED NIGHT

Are we expecting the enemy in the night?
I thought not. Then why is the land so silent dark?
I must be the only one for miles so wide awake –
at this hour no other window shows a light.
Once, for every day there were two short nights.
You put out the candles, fell early into the black,
the seamless, dreamless, bottomless sack, then woke
midway to tend your stock, rekindle lights.
Why do we hope to sleep the whole night through?
And 3.00 a.m. is a fine time to receive your friends,
make love, conduct business, meditate and pray
before going back to bed for the night, part two.
A moonlit walk, cool grass beneath bare feet lends
peace to contemplation of the coming day.

The Light from the West

LOOPS

It is 3.30 in Liverpool
a Wednesday, the day before St Patrick's Day
and I take time in the sun on my way to the library
because tonight there's poetry on Hope Street
but I don't know if my friends will come.

So I sit on a cube, light a cigarette and begin to write
while I watch passers-by – the way some move on
how others drift – when time loops back because
I see Khadeja crossing Williamson Square
in her black hijab and Bogart raincoat. She walks fast
talking with a sister – no, a daughter – then ten years concertina
and I'm right on the edge of calling out Khadeja!
as the distance between us stretches like a desert and I'm blown away
thinking maybe she's forgotten but when I look again
Khadeja and her daughter have gone.

Then I notice how in springtime
the fountains dance a different way to Christmas
when it was all fine mist in the late-night shopping darkness
but today we have arches looping a pergola outside Pronuptia
and a laughing child in cherry leggings zigzags through hoops
of spray.
And the square is full of birds!
Pigeons strut and coo and peck around my feet and the fragile stems of saplings
and gulls wheel and scream overhead while the sun sinks low over Sayers'
and one blue taxi waits alone on the rank. A letter has fallen
from the sign above Stoniers' leaving HINA for CHINA
and a couple beside me on the cube get entangled in kisses
then a girl with palomino hair and pin stripes click clacks by
whispering to a lover locked inside her mobile
and I become invisible in the molten light.

The Light from the West

I leave for the Central Library. It is 4.19.
But I'm wondering about time as in rivers
how it meanders on without us –
about you and me and Khadeja and how much longer
before your ghost moves on forever.

The Light from the West

THE SPACES IN BETWEEN

bright patches contract, reveal a deeper green
as light backs out of my garden like someone
painting herself into a corner
darkness taking over, eating up the sun
in the spaces in between

clouds move faster, the shift of light and shade
flickers in a time-lapse film, all action compressed
or an old movie, over-cranked
projected on a silver screen
Air Force Blue, Wedgwood, cobalt
in the spaces in between

this house could break loose from Earth
rise above fields and woods and on and on
up past office blocks, high towers and spires
a weather station climbing to the stratosphere

or a ketch which having slipped her moorings
rides unskippered over walls of water
whip-cracks and moans as she enters
the dark latitudes of winter
oceans of ice and howling
in the spaces in between

frail summer chairs fold in on themselves
some utterly collapsed, they face all ways
in a disordered conversation
the chat that turned into a fight
in the spaces in between

The Light from the West

great red leaves the size of paper plates
fly past my upper windows
lily pads mottle yellow, rot
retreat to roots in the depths of the pond
fronds of willow stream horizontal on the charged air
yet the branches flex and bend with the gusts
and webs remain unbroken
in the spaces in between

if autumn means mist and melancholia
and winter the sleep of nature
where does this wild power come from?
the wind is a madman on the run from the asylum
hiding from capture
in the spaces in between

AUDIT AT THE BREAKFAST BAR

One table lamp, dimmable to suit mood.
Digital radio, stations preset, like me now in my ways.
The List, a work in progress as time outsprints me.
To trek to Isfahan? The mosques, that fabled square?
Remember to put the rubbish out tonight.
Keys in a saucer, spares and those held for neighbours,
as they hold mine, in trust – and the new, unspoken fear
of a fall from a ladder, a slip in the shower.
Who would miss me? Find me? How long?
Small, local paper dramas, unconsidered before.
One contacts book, leaves loose and bloated
through coffee spills and wear, some names
blurred where blue-black ink has run.
Others lost now to drift. Or death.
A sheaf of pens, stuffed in a pot, some current,
others mute or stuttering, waiting for the miracle
gush of fluency. Bottle of anti-inflammatories
to dull the bitching housemaid's knee.

These are stalwart, my unsung back-room boys.
But pity the transients, the accidentals passing through
who rarely reach their destination. But at least set out
with such enthusiasm in the planning.
Fogged binoculars, fetched down from the loft
to observe a lone magpie bouncing in the rain.
Copper coins, counted and bagged, that never quite make it
as far as the bank. The unbroached jar of beeswax
(my fine intentions of sheen on bookshelves).
Unsown seeds waiting for the soil to warm.

The Light from the West

And *Maneki Neko*, bringer of good fortune,
his plastic paw stilled, not beckoning,
lacking the battery I keep forgetting.

Maneki Neko: Statuette of a waving or beckoning cat (depending on the turn of paw) and thought to bring good luck and prosperity. Often seen in Chinese restaurants though of Japanese origin.

NO THRILLS

So what if you've become, in the Newspeak, 'risk-averse'?
No thrills in losing your shirt, the house – or worse –
on some fragile, wild-eyed horse,
toss of dice, roulette's caprice.

You don't even trust yourself to park on the roof
of a multi-storey. Or stroll a windswept cliff-top.
Suppose you stepped just a little further out,
beguiled by that inner siren voice:

What if I ...?

Don't ever ride The Wild Mouse, Nemesis, The Twilight Zone.
You get nervy in the topsy-turvy world of pleasure parks after dark,
those ink-black voids beckoning beyond the lights,
dread the loud, relentless, driving beat, the looming crowds
of cackling women, larky girls and mad, bad boys.
All that noise and heat and sweat.
You've never had the nous for flight
nor the guts to stay and fight
when it all kicks off.

No more late-night horror flicks on TV.
Why scare yourself half to death for a quick
frisson down the spine? Why court a heart attack
to prove you're still alive?

Double-bolt the back door, unplug the telly, warm the milk.
Dullness is all. Lie down beside me. Try to sleep.
And if the axeman calls tonight,
let him tear his hair and weep.

COLD WAR

The snow lies deep and white as the pillow
muffling Free Europe on my radio –
Reds under the beds of American children,
gremlins plotting in the halls of the Kremlin –
Midnight in Moscow.

So, toot your trumpet, Kenny. Blow, man, blow.
Down in the salt mines it's forty below –
so rip up a storm, you suave young Jazzmen
while the snow lies deep

on prairie and steppe, our secret silos.
Do submarines lurk beneath the ice floes,
missiles poised to ignite Armageddon,
blast us to hell in full sight of heaven?
1962, midnight in Moscow,
and the snow lies deep.

The Light from the West

EXPLORERS

(after Julia Copus, originator of the specular form)

Castaway explorers, every one of us
bleached like driftwood on a dangerous island –
are we jetsam, strange relics pocked and pitted, washed up
needing to know how much we are treasured?
We keep the old sea chest locked but empty,
leached of all colour, as a reminder
of how things in those days were.
Its contents moulder in a forgotten museum
somewhere down an alley in a foreign city.
This is one reason for losing the past
and everything it holds.
Now we own the whole blue gorgeous world,
we've seen further than voyagers to other stars.
Wondering at how far out we've been
staring the thousand yard stare, you pull me to you
as I step back from the beckoning edge.
The surf hammers the rocks below.

The surf hammers the rocks below
as I step back from the beckoning edge
staring the thousand yard stare. You pull me to you
wondering at how far out we've been;
we've seen further than voyagers to other stars
now we own the whole blue gorgeous world
and everything it holds.
This is one reason for losing the past
somewhere down an alley in a foreign city.
Its contents moulder in a forgotten museum
of how things in those days were
leached of all colour. As a reminder
we keep the old sea chest locked but empty,
needing to know how much we are treasured.

The Light from the West

Are we jetsam, strange relics pocked and pitted, washed up
bleached like driftwood on a dangerous island –
castaway explorers, every one of us?

ESCAPE PLAN

I'm watching Selwyn   in the expanding dawn
restless night   half-light united in
insomniacs' delight   brewing coffee
feeding cats   toast in flames
shipping forecast   up not dressed
He steps out immaculate   full country fig
deerstalker bamboo cane   to walk the dog
off its last legs   down tangled lanes
Selwyn   walks alone

Selwyn's watching   a sea of green corn
tall swaying slightly   in the breeze
with misty bloodshot   submariner's eyes
scans a distant   Pacific Ocean
sees a tell-tale   ripple winging
a lifetime ago   the silver torpedo
bulkheads booming   comrades drifting
bringing a hero home   unregarded now
Selwyn tipples alone

They're watching Selwyn   wanderly driving
his heavy-handed   steady Jag yonderly
puttering for petrol   boy racer of Brooklands
lost on a B road   pit stops of the mind
oily rag evoking   loud howling of engines
sparks flying   the chequered flag
black acrid choking   wreckage smoking
two aces up   his smouldering sleeve
Selwyn ponders alone

She's watching Selwyn   thinks it's Walter Mitty
shrill bitter pretty woman   doll-like in her garden
pets moon-crazy hares   cold concrete herons
frets over vet's bills   falling thick and fast

The Light from the West

as papery leaves   on friends departed
no warning cramps   damp night chills
sombre suits huddle   under black gamps
approaching storms   cloud Selwyn's morning
Selwyn broods alone

The Moon's watching Selwyn   gazing stars uncharted
voids and ills fill   endless finite days yet
I've been watching closely lately   and I've seen
a brave red shirt   blazing after funerals
returned his voyager's wave   marked the exchange
of brogues for deckshoes   true colours shown
freedom soon   in this soft scape
coasting loose   with a warm wind blowing
Selwyn sails alone

MISCELLANEOUS

RED COYOTES

The coyotes of Mars grow long red fur,
sleep whole days away in volcano craters,
the wiliest of them can throw their voices
so you can never be absolutely certain sure
exactly where they are ...

till a sound like crazy laughter
or the red winds howling in the evening
goes echoing through the mountains,
bouncing off the canyon walls.

At darkfall they go sniffing after water
with bright red whiskers bristling
and fine red tails quivering
like compass needles, flickering.

They work in packs
fanning out across dead plains,
round steep ragged-edged ravines
while the red planet glows and spins in sleep
coyotes follow deep cracks of dried-up creeks
seeking lost red rivers running far below.

Later prowling the labyrinth of night
they move on silent tips of small red paws
leaving very faint tracks indeed
these read:

We are red dogs in red dust.
Sometimes we fight, sometimes we play
till whirlwinds scatter our spoor.
But always we are dogs in dust.

The Light from the West

It catches them always wistful
to watch the ghostly blue-green earthrise,
their eyes stinging with ammonia,
they curl in dusty craters
to sleep and dream of paradise
their lost land, America.

SWALLOW DIVER

(after Julia Copus, originator of the specular form)

The swallow diver leaves only ripples.
Again and again he pierces the skin of the lido and
an image into my mind – a stiletto: clean, swift and silent –
sunlight glances off the blade of his body, so slim, milltown
pale. It's August and I'm burning
to tell him he's the most graceful creature I've ever seen.
His long dark hair dripping water like raindrops on the hot
pitted concrete, I want
to smooth the hair of this beautiful boy with the jutting
Adam's apple. I watch
taut outstretched arms lift him up and out into the empty air.
Too late.
As if in slow motion, he rises, glistening, out of the blue;
transfixed, the crowd watch
his head, neck and shoulders, the arch of his back, the curve of
his rump roll over.
As if through some substance neither air nor water but viscous,
heavy as oil or resin
he falls, twisting, tumbling down, down. Someone says *He's
dead. Don't look* but I do.
A domino wave of silence washes over the lido – the silence,
leaden
you notice when wings stop beating.

You notice when wings stop beathing.
A domino wave of silence washes over the lido. The silence.
Leaden
he falls, twisting, tumbling down, down. Someone says *He's
dead. Don't look*. But I do
as if through some substance neither air nor water but viscous,
heavy as oil or resin.

The Light from the West

His head, neck and shoulders, the arch of his back, the curve
of his rump roll over.
As if in slow motion, he rises, glistening, out of the blue.
Transfixed, the crowd watch
taut outstretched arms lift him up and out into the empty air.
Too late,
to smooth the hair of this beautiful boy with the jutting
Adam's apple – I watch
his long dark hair dripping water like raindrops on the hot
pitted concrete. I want
to tell him he's the most graceful creature I've ever seen.
Sunlight glances off the blade of his body. So slim. Milltown
pale. It's August and I'm burning
an image into my mind. A stiletto: clean, swift and silent.
Again and again he pierces the skin of the lido, and
the swallow diver leaves only ripples.

The Light from the West

FLEROVIUM (UNUNQUADIUM) PERIODIC NUMBER 114

Symbols and formulae at swim on my screen,
Flerovium, cuckoo cypher, sly late entrant at 114
in the Miss Periodic Table Beauty Pageant,
I discover brief celebrity, her questionable kinship
with the noble gases – one more volatile metal
seeking an *island of stability*. No cute ambassador
for world peace but superheavy, radioactive –
her half-life as long as it takes to skim these lines.
She lacks chutzpah, pazzazz, magnesium's fizzing flare;
the stamina of iron; the allure and influence of gold.
Economies will not rise and fall on Flerovium's whim.
Ephemeral, elusive element synthesised fleetingly
in the Dubna cyclotron, her *abundances* not found
on earth nor sun, all our closer heavens.

SMALL FOR THE AVERAGE WOMAN

Her hands are small for the average woman
grey, cold and dry to the touch
nail splits hidden under winter pale polish
long thin fingers poke from fingerless gloves
like someone else's bones
on a hot summer whim when her hands are brown
the nails are lacquered electric blue
like the lazuli dragonfly she found
shimmering in the marsh iris
these are the nails that leave fur rippled
where she scratches the backs of cats and others
in the case of the others she leaves no traces
these are hands that were once pious
palms pressed hard together in prayer –
now she thinks these hands have done things
they ought not to have done and left undone others
these are the hands that things come away in
door handles, root systems, other people's pens
these are the hands that let things fall and slip
as careless or reluctant as other hands they've known
these are the hands in the concert hall
moved by brave music to applaud
until they burn red and sting all the way home
these are the hands that painted watercolours
but never got the feel for oils
and now retouch the changing canvass of her face
these are the hands that create and destroy
that love the sift of sand and soil
of salt and sugar and flour
the hands that build and plant and knead
these are the hands of a magpie pirate
attracted to glittering things and old red gold
a Turkish puzzler and a silver wishbone
and her wedding ring now sized down

The Light from the West

these are the hands that can hold cups full of ocean
hailstones, snakes, feel the lightness of wild birds
the power of rain, the smear of dregs and ashes
the possibilities of keys and the allure of foreign coins
thin skinned and etched with fine herringbones
lying in the bath she mourns drowned sailors

MERCY'S MANIKIN

Down in his plantation garden
coxcombs dance in scarlet rows.

With one small hand she takes the bodkin
(how the seed inside her grows!)

the doll wears a coat she cut from sacking,
cotton-cloud hair tied back in a bow.

Mercy, busy in the kitchen,
pricks her thumb so the hatred flows,

then twists the bodkin in the stuffing
where she knows his heart should go.

Soon he will grow pale and sicken,
cry out for Mercy in his woe.

And she will trim a length of linen,
singing softly as she sews.

THREE RIDDLES

Seeming kindly, soft and buttery,
I smooth your features like Vaseline on a lens.
You imagine you'll always find me
close at hand when power and sight are lost.
Dream on. I am inconstant, mercurial,
I rise and fall. I wax and wane.
As soon as illumine, I would cast you
into the black pools that surround you.
Do not be fooled. Though born of heat,
I am cold at heart, a false friend,
peddling cheap romance and flattery.

I love the country more than the city,
seldom visit the coast. I am forever
shrinking and expanding,
changing colour with the light.
Little by little I crumble your mortar,
undermine your structures. I entomb
airmen, climbers in the walls of mountains,
my crystals glitter in a billion stars.

I am all around you, everywhere,
inside your body, in the air,
yet you are always searching for me.
In the wrong place at the wrong time
I might overwhelm you, carry you off,
change state, retreat deep beneath the earth.
I am more precious than gold or oil.
Soon you will murder your brother for me.

INDEX

1000 Lashes	116
A Pact	126
Alien	51
At Bamburgh	62
At Kai's Beach Bar	61
Audit at the Breakfast Bar	146
Autumn at the Villa Cleobolus	11
Before I Remembered	55
Blood Moon	76
Camouflage	21
Cod	81
Cold War	149
Come November	129
Common Weeds Cut-up	123
Conman Autumn	127
Delamere	25
Dog Tag	73
Durban	79
Escape Plan	152
Excavations, Chester	18
Explorers	150
Fetish	38
Finishing School	82
Flerovium (Ununquadium) Periodic Number 114	159
For George	91
For St Elmo	128
For Valerie	45
Freerunners	20
Ghosts at My Table	46
Griffiths Road Lagoons	28
Guttering	90
Hair (1969)	69
Harajuku Lovers	101

Heigh Ho, Silver	98
Helter Skelter Birthday Blues	47
How Tabby Cats Got Their Name	49
Howick Hall, September 2011	8
I Come From	2
In Another Country, Soldiers	19
In Which I, Arturo, Am Likened to an Artichoke	96
Island	86
Isle of the Cross	111
Jazz	133
Journey of the Pilgrims	114
Jubilo	139
Kisses	39
Like Mother, Like Daughter	67
Lime Street Love	34
Liverpool Ghazal	5
Long Grass Sundays	83
Loops	142
Loose Pantoum for Will Self	16
Lotus Eating	121
Margarethe	88
Mary Miller	107
Mercy's Manikin	162
Message From McNaught	137
Miss Thomas	52
Never The Farm	43
No Lullaby	138
No Thrills	148
Northwich Poem/I Always Punched Above My Weight	6
Northwich Under The Skin	3
Nothing To Do With Mother	44
O'Connell Street 1963	80
Old Melon Eyes	50
On Cold Sunday Lunch with Recipe	59
On Shakespeare's 450th Birthday	103
One Night an Iris	95
Pantoum For Autumn	120

Passerine..66
Patchouli...57
Pink...92
Possession..36
Protea..125
Provincial...70
Puffball Roulette...124
Red Coyotes..155
Red Lights..23
River Daughter, River Mother..31
River Irwell Time..132
Rollmops..93
Russian Caravan...105
Salt and Vinegar...41
Sargasso Soup...12
Shalimar and Ether..63
Silkweed...77
Slow..72
Small for the Average Woman..160
Something of the Night...135
Sprawl..118
Squire's Gate Airport...15
Starlings...122
Swallow Diver...157
Sweet William...10
The Archaeology of Tiramisu...65
The Ballad of 'Lucky' Tower...109
The Bridge...22
The Divided Night...141
The Drawer Less Opened..85
The Geologist's iPad..60
The Hand Colourist...58
The House Cat..53
The Hunger Says..42
The Paradise Project..29
The Shadow Flyers...113
The Spaces In Between..144

These Old People	30
Three Riddles	163
Thurstaston	17
Time	78
Today Is Not a Day for Poetry	54
Tzarina	104
Valentine Ghazal	35
Visitors 1st August 2003	26
Waiting for Rain	119
West Kirby	14
Wild Horses	37
Winter Sleepwalking	130

Printed in Dunstable, United Kingdom